# Marshall McLuhan

# Counter blast

Designed by Harley Parker

Harcourt, Brace & World, Inc.    New York

Good taste is the first refuge of the witless.

Harley Parker

In 1914, a few weeks before the war, there appeared from the Rebel Art Center in London, BLAST. Wyndham Lewis, the painter, was the perpetrator of this blast. The word is a jest derived from blastoderm, a term from embryology. Lewis also had reference to the GERM, the Art magazine put out by the Rossetti Circle. BLAST, typographically, is unique in the history of English literature. Lewis told me that he had found it impossible to get it set up by any London printer whatever. He finally found an alcoholic ex-printer who agreed to set it up exactly as Lewis required in return for large supplies of liquor. Nearly the entire magazine is set up in heavy headline type. Headlines are icons, not literature.

Certainly the present work makes no claim to be literature, but it is just as difficult now as in the time of Lewis to get any prose or verse set up in headline type.

In 1954 Wyndham Lewis blasted Toronto in the novel SELF-CONDEMNED. His Rene (reborn) seeking his true spiritual self selects Toronto, Momaco (Mom & Co.), as a colonial cyclotron in which to explore his human ego. He succeeds in annihilating himself.

In AMERICA AND COSMIC MAN Lewis saw North America as a benign rock-crusher in which all remnants of European nationalism and individualism were happily reduced to cosmic baby powder. The new media are blowing a lot of the baby powder around the pendant cradle of the New Man today. The dust gets in our eyes.

The term COUNTERBLAST does not imply any attempt to erode or explode BLAST. Rather it indicates the need for a counter-environment as a means of perceiving the dominant one. Today we live invested with an electric information environment that is quite as imperceptible to us as water is to a fish. At the beginning of his work, Pavlov found that the conditioning of his dogs depended on a previous conditioning. He placed one environment within another one. Such is COUNTER-BLAST.

*Marshall McLuhan*

BLAST

```
?????
?????
?????
 ?????
 ?????
  ?????
  ?????
   ?????
    ?????
    ?????
     ?????
      ?????
       ?????
        ?????
         ?????
          ?????
           ?????
            ?????
       the    ?????
             ?????
              ?????
    printed    ?????
               ?????
      page     ?????
                ?????
                 ?????
                  ?????
                   ?????
                    ?????
                     ?????
                      ?????
                       ?????
                        ?????
                         ?????
                          ?????
                           ?????
                            ?????
                             ????
                              ???
                               ??
                                ?
```

# FRENCH CANADIAN

for keeping

D THE BREATH · THE HAND THAT SIGNED THE PAPER FELLED THE CITY

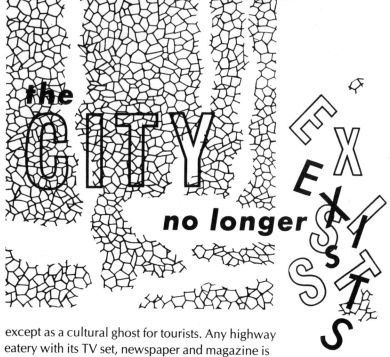

# the CITY
## no longer
# EXISTS

except as a cultural ghost for tourists. Any highway eatery with its TV set, newspaper and magazine is as cosmopolitan as New York or Paris.

The peasant was always a suburban parasite. The farmer no longer exists; today he is a "city" man.

The metropolis today is a classroom; the ads are its teachers. The traditional classroom is an obsolete detention home, a feudal dungeon.

## *the city*
## *is obsolete*

EX CIT.

## ASK
## THE COMPUTER

It is to the urb what LSD is to the electronic yokel; that is, it ends all goals and objectives and points of view.

The **INSTANTANEOUS** global coverage of radio-TV make the city form meaningless, functionless. Cities were once related to the realities of production and intercommunication. Not now.

Until **WRITING** was invented, we lived in acoustic space, where all backward peoples still live: boundless, directionless, horizonless, the dark of the mind, the world of emotion, primordial intuition, mafia-ridden. Speech is a social chart of this dark bog.

**SPEECH** structures the abyss of mental and acoustic space, shrouding the race; it is a cosmic, invisible architecture of the human dark.

In the computer age, speech yields to macrocosmic gesticulation or the direct interface of total cultures. The silent movies began this move.

that I may SEE you.

SPEAK

**Are you tongue blind?**

**WRITING** turned a spotlight on the high, dim Sierras of speech; writing was the visualization of acoustic space. It lit up the dark.

A goose quill put an end to talk, abolished mystery, gave us enclosed space and towns, brought roads and armies and bureaucracies. It was the basic metaphor with which the cycle of **CIVILIZATION** began, the step from the dark into the light of the mind. The hand that filled a paper built a city.

The handwriting is on the celluloid walls of Hollywood; the Age of Writing has passed. We must invent a **NEW METAPHOR**, restructure our thoughts and feelings. The new media are not bridges between man and nature:

# they are nature.

BLESS

Advertising Art

for its PICTORIAL

VERBAL

vitality and creativity

**Movies and TV** complete the cycle of mechanization of the human sensorium. With the omnipresent ear and moving eye, we have abolished the dynamics of Western civilization.

WE ARE BACK IN ACOUSTIC SPACE

WE ARE BACK IN ACOUSTIC SPACE

We begin again to structure the primordial feelings and emotions from which 3000 years of literacy divorced us. We begin again to live a myth.

**PHOTOGRAPHY** was the mechanization of the perspective painting and of the arrested eye; it broke the barriers of the nationalist, vernacular space created by printing. Printing upset the balance of oral and written speech; photography upset the balance of ear and eye.

**TELEPHONE, PHONOGRAPH** and **RADIO** are the mechanization of post-literate acoustic space. Radio returns us to the dark of the mind, to the invasions from Mars and Orson Welles; it mechanizes the well of loneliness that is acoustic space: the human heart-throb put on a PA system provides a well of loneliness in which anyone can drown.

By surpassing writing, we have regained our sensorial WHOLENESS, not on a national or cultural plane, but on a cosmic plane. We have evoked a super-civilized sub-primitive man.

NOBODY yet knows the languages inherent in the new technological culture; we are all technological idiots in terms of the new situation. Our most impressive words and thoughts betray us by referring to the previously existent, not to the present.

The MECHANIZATION of writing mechanized the visual-acoustic metaphor on which all civilization rests; it created the classroom and mass education, the modern press and telegraph. It was the original assembly-line. Gutenberg made all history available as classified data: the transportable book brought the world of the dead into the space of the gentleman's library; the telegraph brought the entire world of the living to the workman's breakfast table.

The **INSTANTANEOUS** global coverage of radio-TV make the city form meaningless, functionless. Cities were once related to the realities of production and intercommunication. Not now.

Until **WRITING** was invented, we lived in acoustic space, where all backward peoples still live: boundless, directionless, horizonless, the dark of the mind, the world of emotion, primordial intuition, mafia-ridden. Speech is a social chart of this dark bog.

**SPEECH** structures the abyss of mental and acoustic space, shrouding the race; it is a cosmic, invisible architecture of the human dark.

In the computer age, speech yields to macrocosmic gesticulation or the direct interface of total cultures. The silent movies began this move.

that I may SEE you.

SPEAK

**Are you tongue blind?**

**WRITING** turned a spotlight on the high, dim Sierras of speech; writing was the visualization of acoustic space. It lit up the dark.

A goose quill put an end to talk, abolished mystery, gave us enclosed space and towns, brought roads and armies and bureaucracies. It was the basic metaphor with which the cycle of **CIVILIZATION** began, the step from the dark into the light of the mind. The hand that filled a paper built a city.

The handwriting is on the celluloid walls of Hollywood; the Age of Writing has passed. We must invent a **NEW METAPHOR**, restructure our thoughts and feelings. The new media are not bridges between man and nature:

# they are nature.

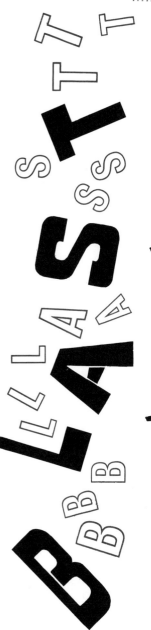

# The Sports Page

**pantheon of pickled
gods and archetypes**

# The Comic Strip

**upholder of
HOMERIC CULTURE**

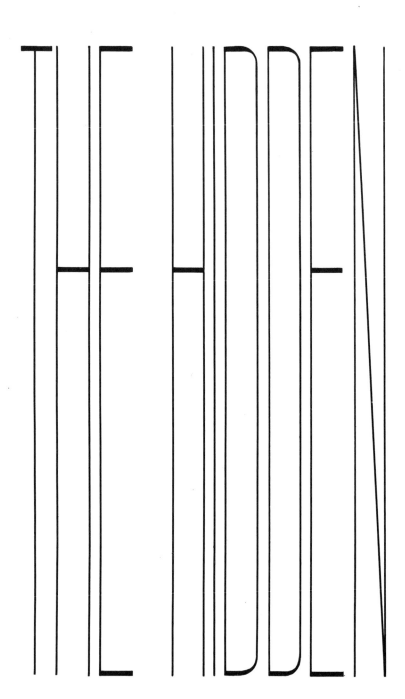

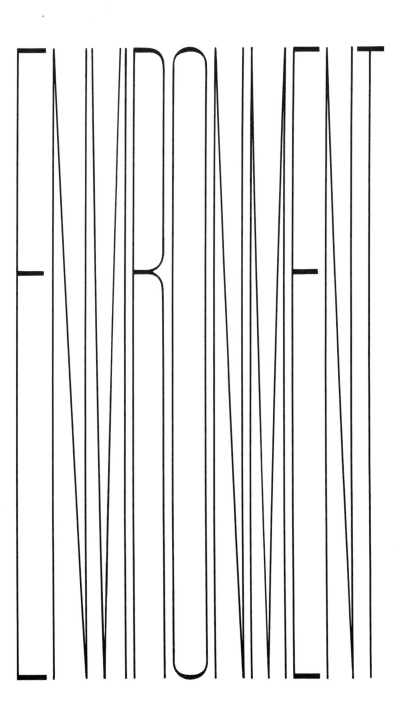

Until now, all media have been given the <u>flat earth approach</u> — that is, to common sense, the earth is flat. To private, <u>unaided</u> perception, it must always seem flat. Media of all kinds exert no effect on ordinary perception. They merely serve human ends (like chairs!) and convey data, etc. But macroscopically, the content fades and the medium itself looms large, as does earth to the astronaut. A stretch of time provides for media the macroscopic distance that the telescope does for the heavens.

Media effects are new environments as imperceptible as water to a fish, subliminal for the most part. Freud's censor is the mechanism by which in sensation we protect ourselves from over-stimulation. We live in the rear-view mirror.

Media tend to isolate one or another sense from the others. The result is hypnosis. The other extreme is withdrawing of sensation with resulting hallucination as in dreams or DT's, etc. But non-phonetic writing does not isolate senses. Tactility is not a sense but an interplay of all senses.

Any medium, by dilating sense to fill the whole field, creates the necessary conditions of hypnosis in that area. This explains why at no time has any culture been aware of the effect of its media on its overall association, not even retrospectively.

## THE MEDIUM IS THE MESS AGE

means the sensory effect of the environments created by innovations, for example the effect of writing on speech. The content of writing is speech; but the content of speech is mental dance, nonverbal ESP. The content of film is a collection of media within media. The "message" is all of them at once.

SPEECHASENCODEDVISUALLYINWRITINGISNOTSPEECH
ANYLONGER. It is given a visual bias of great intensity by
being reduced to writing. Moreover, as written, it's abstracted from all other senses. Speech on radio is similarly
reduced to one sense: the auditory-aural. Radio is not
speech though it seems, like writing, to "contain" speech.
Our illusion of "content" derives from one medium being
"within" or simultaneous with another. For this reason in-
strumental music has no "content" and non-objective art
likewise is an abstract manipulation of the modalities of
sight.

Multi-screen projection tends to end the story-line, as the
symbolist poem ends narrative in verse. That is, multiple
screen in creating a simultaneous syntax eliminates the
literary medium from film.

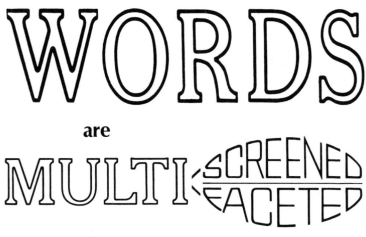

**WORDS** are **MULTI-SCREENED-FACETED** but simultaneous myths.

They are complex processes. *"Sea shell ebb music way-
river she flows."*

The Addison-Steele discovery of **equitone** prose, in addition to creating a fixed point of view, enabled the author to become a "man of letters". He could now approach the large, homogenized public of a market society in a consistent and complacent role.

That is, the maintaining of supercilious equitone and attitude to an audience equals Mandarin or Bloomsbury prose. This is the origin of the "man of letters." Till the discovery of equitone prose, the writer had to wear a corporate, tribal mask of some sort, as did Swift. The medieval clown dominates the role of writer until the Addison-Steele discovery of mass-production flow of equitone.

This all ended with the symbolist recovery of tribal, collective awareness: *Hypocrite lecteur.*

# Is the déjà vu phenomenon, i.e. "I've been here before", exotic with the "man of letters", and normal and unnoticed by non-literate man?

If so, it could account for the deep, reincarnational or déjà vu sense of the non-literate societies.

The sensation itself may result from situations of deep sensuous *involvement,* natural in highly tactual cultures and environments. *Ergo* normal in childhood. May this not be the source of the *abiding* sense of reincarnation in non-literate societies, and explain the lack of such sensation in literate societies? It should be possible to create physical situations in which *anybody* might experience the sensation of *déjà vu.*

Young people who have experienced a decade of TV (to cite only the most obvious mosaic form of the electric age) have naturally imbibed an urge towards involvement in depth that makes all the remote and visualized goals of visual culture seem not only unreal but irrelevant, and not only irrelevant but anaemic. It's the total involvement in all-inclusive nowness that occurs in young lives via TV's mosaic image. This change in attitude has nothing to do with programming in any way, and would be the same if the programs consisted entirely of the highest cultural content. The change in attitude resulting from relating themselves to the mosaic TV image would occur in any event. The TV child expects involvement and doesn't want a specialist *job* in the future. He does want a *role* and deep commitment to his society. Unbridled and misunderstood, this richly human need can manifest itself in the distorted forms portrayed in *West Side Story*.

**work** = fragmented task and consequent non-involvement of whole person. The executive as dropout.

**leisure** = involvement, as in hobbies or in conversation. Where involvement is high, work is low.

When the whole man moves into a specialist area he is a clown. Hence the appeal of the comics. Clowns are integral. Every society has an acrobatic area for specialists. The clown in any society is what is left over, unused, from this acrobatic high-wire act. His act is to attempt the high-wire or specialty, using human *wholeness*. Even walking is made to appear a crazy aberration of pedantic minds.

TV children have lived several lifetimes by the time they enter grade 1, just as they have travelled farther by the age of seven than their grandparents ever travelled. The TV adult returns to grade school in order to make possible several new careers for himself. Acceleration of information movement can have, as one of its consequences, a multiplicity of jobs for everybody. Joblessness as the consequence of automation may well mean the end of the single job for the single lifetime, and the switchover to a multiplicity of jobs for every lifetime.

BLESS

THE BEATLES

FOR REAFFIRMING THAT THE HAND THAT ROCKS THE CRADLE RULES THE

WORLD

BLESS

# ENVIRONMENT IS PROCESS, NOT CONTAINER.

The content of environment gets changed into art form. Environment is always regarded as degrading. Bricks put indoors become art. Food-gathering, when environed by neolithic specialism, becomes art form. Hunting and all things of the chase become snobbish ornaments of the upper crust in the new society. In our time, all mechanical forms are tending to become snobbish art forms, just as a little earlier, all the arts and crafts had become "arty-crafty." The environment always manages somehow to be invisible. Only the content, the preceding environment, is noticeable.

**itself became content, having had a short reign as environment.**

Technologies begin as anti-environments, as controls, and then become environmental, needing the endless spawning of new anti-environments as controls. Dreams are anti-environment for physiological sleep. Private consciousness is anti-environment for collective unconscious as environment.

# TENSIONS MAN ARE THE HOMINIZATION OF THE WORLD.

## It is a nd PHASE OF THE ORIGINAL CREATION

All technologies are collective unconscious. All arts, science and philosophy are anti-environmental controls that are ever merging into the environmental and losing their power to create awareness of environment. When arts fail to cope with the environment by being anti-environment then there can be a shift to a rapid succession of innovations as ersatz anti-environments.

To say that any technology or extension of man creates a new environment is a much better way of saying that the medium is the message. This environment is always "invisible" and its content is always the old technology. The old technology is altered considerably by the enveloping action of the new technology.

**Technologies** would seem to be the pushing of the **archetypal** forms of the **unconscious** out into **social** consciousness. May this not help explain why technology as **environment** is typically **unconscious?** The interplay between environmental and content factors, between old and new technologies, seems to obtain in all fields whatever. In **politics**, the **new conservativism** has as its **content** the old **liberalism**. Every **new** technology requires a **war** in order to recover an **image made** by the **old environment.**

The basic changes of our time lead us towards confronting the **environment** as **artefact.** In a **non-literate** society, there is **no art** in our sense, but the whole **environment** is experienced as **unitary.** Neolithic specialism ended that. The Balinese say: "We have **no art.** We do everything **as well as possible**"; that is, they **program** the **environment** instead of its **content**.

What we call **art** would seem to be **specialist artefacts** for enhancing human **perception**. **Since** the **Renaissance**, the **arts** have become privileged means of **perception for the few**, rather than means of **participation** in a common life, or **environment**. This phase now seems to be ending, except that we are extending the **privileged artefact** principally to the **environment** itself.

Is not this acceptance of the **environment as artefact** part of our drive to improve the **learning process**, instead of concern with the **right content** for learning, the **right environment** for maximizing learning?

In the Hawthorne experiment, instead of saying that **testing falsifies** the **content** or distorts the perceptions of those being tested, might they not have said that **testing** itself is an **ideal environment** for the **learning** process? **Testing** represents a set of **controlled conditions** which in effect **accelerate** and improve **learning and work**. The **tester** is always **unaware** of the environment or **cultural assumptions** of his **procedures**. NASA is **Newtonian**, not **twentieth**-century.

# WHAT WE CALL
# ART
## would seem to be specialist artefacts for enhancing human
# PERCEPTION

IN THE AG
INFORMA

the

man                    fo

returns as
        manthef

Our ecological a
It assumes total i
rather than fragme

An increase in vis
society creates
fragmentation, ci
crease in the sar
involvement, triba
ness, etc.

Circuitry is the er
is the inner trip fo
Each new techno
—is a reprogramm
environment mak
archetype. The n
ceived. We see tl
Only children a
enough to see the

EX
OF

**We're in
an age of**

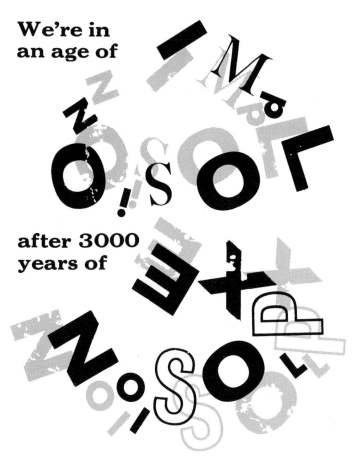

**after 3000
years of**

——————— an implosion in which everybody is involved with everybody. The age of co-presence of all individuals is the age of communication — **the age of instant humans.** Computer data-banks dissolve the human image. **Love thy label as thyself**.

The recent ages have been mechanical. The electric age is organic.

## PRE-LITERATE MAN

outered his whole body in ship or house
or rollers (the Incas had no wheel).

## LITERATE MAN

specialized by outering parts of himself —
e.g., book as compared with movie.

## ELECTRONIC MAN

like pre-literate man, ablates or outers
the whole man. His information environment is his own nervous system.

The electronic age is the age of ecology.
It's the study and projection of the total
environment of organisms and people,
because of the instant coherence of all
factors, made possible by moving information at electric speeds. Such speed of
synchronized information has rendered,
for example, both wheel and assembly-
line obsolescent.

The spectacular rise of information levels
provides predictors of economic growth.
Economic transactions tend more and
more toward the exchange of knowledge
rather than exchange of commodities. War
itself becomes "cold" war in which the
struggle is to alter the image of the enemy
by global information flow. Computer
speed and inclusiveness is LSD for Business—that is, the end of goals and objectives.

With the large rise of information levels, the tendency is for any one natural resource to become a substitute for another. Anything can become fuel; any fuel can become a fabric. The complex reversal which electricity brings to production and the making of wealth is repeated in education, as well as in the arts and sciences. We enter the age of paid learning. Learning itself creates wealth. Education is by many times the largest business in the world.

---

The **Age of Implosion** in education spells the **end of "subjects"** and substitutes instead the **structural study** of the making and **learning process** itself. **Softwear** replaces **hardware**. Witness **London Bridge** and the **Queen Mary**. Any bids for **Big Ben** or the **Leaning Tower**?

# Nothing studied in depth can remain partitioned off as a "subject" in a curriculum.

Today small **children** have begun to study **number theory** and **symbolic logic**. The **world** tends to become a single **classroom** or a non-stop seminar.

In **politics**, the Age of **Implosion** is the **reverse** of **expansion**. We begin to realize the **depth** of our **involvement** in one another as a **total** human **community**.

In the **Age of Information**, media such as **telegraph, telephone, press, photo, radio** and **film** are in themselves new **natural resources** increasing the **wealth** of the community. In the Age of **Information**, the **moving** of information is by many times the **largest business** in the world. Even in the old sense of a business, **moving information** far **outranks** **"heavy" industry**. A T & T alone is much **larger** than **General Motors**.

But the key fact is that it's the **movement of information**, itself, in a kind of non-stop global dialogue that **makes wealth** today. Enrichment has become **automatic** and **total** process; **human chatter** (= jazz) or macroscopic gesticulation supplanting all speech.

All human tools and **technologies**, whether **house** or **wrench** or clothing, **alphabet** or **wheel**, are direct **extensions**, either of the human body or of our **senses**. **Computers** are **extensions** of our **brains**. As **extensions** of our **bodies**, tools and **technologies** give us new **leverage** and new intensity of **perception** and **action**. This they do by a kind of **translation** or **of "applied knowledge."**

# The Old Testament from first to last is a

# COUNTERBLAST

## against all technologies.

**CAIN
SMOTE
THE EARTH
AND THEN
HIS
BROTHER**

**The good guys were all shepherds.**

**VIA COMPUTER**

**man now returns to the shepherd's role.**

**EXTENSIONS OF MAN ARE THE HOMINIZATION OF THE WORLD.**

It is a

**2**nd

**PHASE**

OF THE ORIGINAL

CREATION

# IN THE AGE OF
# INFORMATION

the foodgatherer man returns as manthefactfinder.

Our ecological approach is paleolithic. It assumes total involvement in process rather than fragmentation and detachment.

An increase in visual component in any society creates specialism, alienation, fragmentation, civilization, etc. The decrease in the same, as via TV, creates involvement, tribalization, visceral awareness, etc.

Circuitry is the end of the neolithic age. It is the inner trip for the whole tribe of man. Each new technology — new environment — is a reprogramming of sensory life. A new environment makes the old one into hi-fi archetype. The new one is *always* unperceived. We see the Emperor's *old* clothes. Only children and artists are antisocial enough to see the new ones.

**We're in an age of**

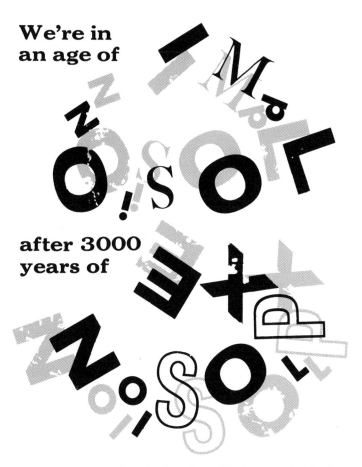

**after 3000 years of**

————— an implosion in which everybody is involved with everybody. The age of co-presence of all individuals is the age of communication — **the age of instant humans.** Computer data-banks dissolve the human image. **Love thy label as thyself**.

The recent ages have been mechanical. The electric age is organic.

## PRE-LITERATE MAN

outered his whole body in ship or house or rollers (the Incas had no wheel).

## LITERATE MAN

specialized by outering parts of himself — e.g., book as compared with movie.

## ELECTRONIC MAN

like pre-literate man, ablates or outers the whole man. His information environment is his own nervous system.

The electronic age is the age of ecology. It's the study and projection of the total environment of organisms and people, because of the instant coherence of all factors, made possible by moving information at electric speeds. Such speed of synchronized information has rendered, for example, both wheel and assembly-line obsolescent.

The spectacular rise of information levels provides predictors of economic growth. Economic transactions tend more and more toward the exchange of knowledge rather than exchange of commodities. War itself becomes "cold" war in which the struggle is to alter the image of the enemy by global information flow. Computer speed and inclusiveness is LSD for Business—that is, the end of goals and objectives.

What we call **art** would seem to be **specialist artefacts** for enhancing human **perception**. **Since** the **Renaissance**, the **arts** have become privileged means of **perception for the few**, rather than means of **participation** in a common life, or **environment**. This phase now seems to be ending, except that we are extending the **privileged artefact** principally to the **environment** itself.

Is not this acceptance of the **environment as artefact** part of our drive to improve the **learning process**, instead of concern with the **right content** for learning, the **right environment** for maximizing learning?

In the Hawthorne experiment, instead of saying that **testing falsifies** the **content** or distorts the perceptions of those being tested, might they not have said that **testing** itself is an **ideal environment** for the **learning** process? **Testing** represents a set of **controlled conditions** which in effect **accelerate** and improve **learning and work**. The **tester** is always **unaware** of the environment or **cultural assumptions** of his **procedures**. NASA is **Newtonian**, not **twentieth**-century.

# WHAT WE CALL

# ART

## would seem to be specialist artefacts for enhancing human

# PERCEPTION

All technologies are collective unconscious. All arts, science and philosophy are anti-environmental controls that are ever merging into the environmental and losing their power to create awareness of environment. When arts fail to cope with the environment by being anti-environment then there can be a shift to a rapid succession of innovations as ersatz anti-environments.

> To say that any technology or extension of man creates a new environment is a much better way of saying that the medium is the message. This environment is always "invisible" and its content is always the old technology. The old technology is altered considerably by the enveloping action of the new technology.

**Technologies** would seem to be the pushing of the **archetypal** forms of the **unconscious** out into **social** consciousness. May this not help explain why technology as **environment** is typically **unconscious?** The interplay between environmental and content factors, between old and new technologies, seems to obtain in all fields whatever. In **politics**, the **new conservativism** has as its **content** the old **liberalism.** Every **new** technology requires a **war** in order to recover an **image made** by the **old environment.**

The basic changes of our time lead us towards confronting the **environment** as artefact. In a **non-literate** society, there is **no art** in our sense, but the whole **environment** is experienced as **unitary.** Neolithic specialism ended that. The Balinese say: "We have **no art.** We do everything **as well as possible''**; that is, they **program** the **environment** instead of its **content.**

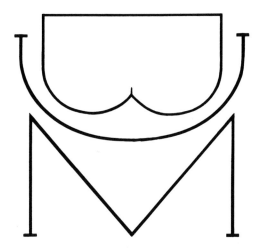

# A chair outers
# the human posterior.

The squat posture is "translated" into a new matter, namely wood or stone or steel. The temporary tension of squatting is translated and fixed in a new matter. The fixing of the human posture in solid matter is a great saver of toil and tension. This is true of all media and tools and technologies. But chair at once causes something else to happen that would never occur without chair.

## A table is born. Table is a further outer-
ing or extension of body resulting from chair. The new fixed posture of chair calls forth a new inclination of body and new needs for the placing of implements and stirring of food. But table also calls forth new arrangements of people at table. The fixing of a posture of the body in a chair has a whole series of consequences.

A wheel is the outering of feet. Feet in rapid rotation constitute the "rotary" action. Much transportation by foot could suggest the action of "wheel" either to the porter or the potter. Today the wheel is obsolescent because the speed of movement now tends to make its action irrelevant. A plane needs wheels when it slows down.

But as with the chair, the wheel at once gave rise to another form of technology: road. As the table altered social patterns, so did the road. The least technology makes a new environment.

The effect of extending the central nervous system is not to create a world-wide city of ever-expanding dimensions but rather a global village of ever-contracting size. "The urb it orbs," Joyce noted.

# To the blind all things are sudden.

The **speed** of **information** movement in the **global village** means that every **human action** or event **involves everybody** in the village **in** the consequences of **every event**. The **new** human **settlement** in terms of the contracted global village has to take into account the **new factor** of **total involvement** of each of us in the **lives** and actions **of all**. In the **age of electricity** and **automation**, the globe becomes a community of **continuous learning**, a single campus in which **everybody**, irrespective of age, is **involved in learning a living**.

In the global village of **continuous learning** and of **total participation** in the human **dialogue**, the problem of settlement is to **extend consciousness** itself and to **maximize** the opportunities of **learning**. The **problems** of settlement in the **earlier mechanical age**, which many seem to suppose are still with us, were utterly **different**. **Then** the problem was to **act** as far as possible **without involving** oneself in the lives of **others**. The **industrial age** gave us a kind of **theatre of the absurd**, in which people trained themselves to **act without reacting**, priding themselves on their **powers of detachment** and **non-involvement**. Ours is the **Age of Implosion**, of **inclusive consciousness** and deep personal involvement. The **crisis** in human settlement arises from a **clash** between these two **opposed forms** of **culture and technology**.

# AGAIN.

**Extensions** of man are **not** so much physic as **psychic** in character. They may even be, as Norman Brown insists, **"neurotic sublimations."** All are **amplifications** of some **special faculty.** Thus they **alter** the whole **complex.**

Throughout **previous evolution,** as it were, we have **protected** the **central nervous system** by **outering** this or that **physical organ** in **tools, housing, clothing, cities.** But each **outering** of individual **organs** was also an **acceleration** and intensification of the general **environment** until the **central nervous system did a flip.** We turned turtle. The **shell** went **inside,** the **organs outside.** Turtles with **soft shells** become **vicious.** That's our **present state.** But when an **organ goes out** (ablation), it goes **numb.** The central nervous system has gone **numb,** for **survival,** i.e., we enter the **age of the unconscious** with **electronics,** and **consciousness** shifts to the **physical organs,** even in the body **politic.** There is great **stepping up of physical awareness** and a **big drop in mental awareness** when the **central nervous system** goes **outward.**

**Language** was the **first outering of the central nervous system.** In **language** we put **all** of **ourselves outside.** Then we **retracted** and began to hedge our bets by putting out **single senses** like **wheel** (feet), **hammer** (fist), **knife** (teethnail), **drum** (ear), **writing** (eye). **Each** of these **altered** both private and corporate **images, creating** great **pain** and **alienation.**

The **one area** which is **numb and unconscious** is the area which **receives the impact.** Thus there is an **exact parallel** with **ablation** in **experimental medicine,** but in **medical ablation** observation is properly **directed, not** to the **numb** area, but to all the **other organs** as they are **affected** by the **numbing** or ablation of the **single organ.**

# BLESS THE ELECTRIC RETURN

## TO THE TRIBAL PALEOLITHIC AGE,
## TO THE WORLD OF THE HUNTER
### AFTER THE

**NEOLITHIC**

**PLANTER**

bless the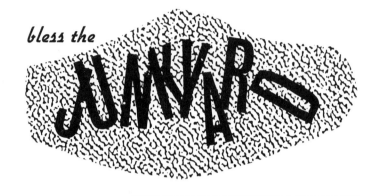

*Lyricist*

**who sighed by sign**

*Help beautify junkyards—throw something lovely away today.*

**bless**

GLENNGOULD

for throwing the

# Concert
# Audience

*into the*

type

drawing    newspaper

tape

Magazines    .    pictogram

language    manuscript

phonograph

PRINT

camera    television

Speech

Books

etc.

# media log

## THE BOOK ARRIVES TOO LATE

About 1830 Lamartine pointed to the newspaper as the end of book culture:

At the same time Dickens used the press as base for a new impressionist art which D. W. Griffiths and Sergei Eisenstein studied in 1920 as the foundation of movie art.

Robert Browning took the newspaper as art model for his impressionist epic *The Ring and the Book;* Mallarmé did the same in *Un Coup de Dés.*

Edgar Poe, a press man and, like Shelley, a science fictioneer, correctly analysed the poetic process. Conditions of newspaper serial publication led both him and Dickens to the process of writing backwards. This means simultaneity of all parts of a composition. Simultaneity compels sharp focus on *effect* of thing made. The artist starts with the effect. Simultaneity is the form of the press in dealing with Earth City. Simultaneity is formula for the writing of both detective story and symbolist poem. These are derivatives (one "low" and one "high") of the new technological culture.

# Joyce's Ulysses

## completed the cycle of this technological art form.

Technological culture in the newspaper form structures ordinary unawareness in patterns which correspond to the most sophisticated manoeuvers of mathematical physics and modern painting.

Newton's *Optics* created the techniques of picturesque and romantic poetry. NASA is Newtonian and obsolete in its program.

In 1830, due to this technological revolution, English popular consciousness was structured in ways which French and European intellectuals did not acquire until a later generation. The Spanish are getting it now: but backward countries start with the latest technologies, by-passing the earlier ones. Witness the American colonies in the eighteenth century.

The Swiss cultural historian Siegfried Giedion has had to invent the concept of "anonymous history" in order to write an account of the new technological culture in Anglo-Saxondom.

The professoriat has turned its back on culture for 200 years because the high culture of technological society is popular culture and knows no boundaries between high and low. There is no longer a gap between business and culture or military and civilian life.

The children of technological man respond with untaught delight to the poetry of trains, ships, planes, and to the beauty of machine products. In the school room officialdom suppresses all their natural experience; children are divorced from their culture. They are not permitted to approach the traditional heritage of mankind through the door of technological awareness; this only possible door for them is slammed in their faces.

Perhaps underestimating the ease of fulfilment, T. S. Eliot said he would prefer an illiterate audience, for the ways of official literacy do not equip the young to know themselves, the past or the present. A parallel is the fact that the white man creates the negro. He creates a world into which natives cannot fit.

The technique of an Eliot poem is a direct application of the method of the popular radio-tube grid circuit to the shaping and control of the charge of meaning. An Eliot poem is one instance of a direct means of experiencing, under conditions of artistic control, the ordinary awareness and culture of contemporary man.

Photography and cinema have abolished realism as too easy; they substitute themselves for realism. They are non-verbal languages.

All the new media, including the press, are art forms which have the power of imposing, like poetry, their own assumptions. The new media are not ways of relating us to the old "real" world; they are the real world and they reshape what remains of the old world at will.

Official culture still strives to force the new media to do the work of the old media. But the horseless carriage did not do the work of the horse; it abolished the horse and did what the horse could never do.

# HORSES are FINE so are BOOKS

# TECHNO-LOGICAL ART

ART takes the whole earth and its population as its material, not as its form.

It is too late to be frightened or disgusted, to greet the unseen with a sneer. Ordinary life-work demands that we harness and subordinate the media to human ends.

The media are not toys; they should not be in the hands of Mother Goose and Peter Pan executives. They can be entrusted only to new artists, because they are art forms that is, new ways of perception, new probes into the world like new species. Evolution as process has shifted from biology to technology. The resulting acceleration of evolution is like a time-capsule.

# HARNESSING THE

is kid stuff
compared to
curbing the

## MOVIE, PRESS OR TELEVISION

The wild broncos of technological culture have yet to find their busters or masters. They have found only their P.T. Barnums. Pat Pauslen would do a better job as a media shepherd than the Madison Avenue infants.

# EUROPEANS CANNOT

master these new powers of technology because they take themselves too seriously and too sentimentally. Europeans cannot imagine the Earth City. They have occupied old city spaces too long to be able to sense the new spaces created by the new media.

# THE ENGLISH

have lived longer with technological culture than anybody else, but they lost their chance to shape it when the ship yielded to the plane. But the English language is already the base of all technology.

The Russians are impotent to shape technological culture because of their inwardness and grimness. The future masters of technology will have to be lighthearted and intelligent. The machine easily masters the grim and the dumb.

AT THE PRESENT TIME

RUSSIAN

AMERICA

LIFE AND POLICY BY VIRTUE OF TECHNOLOGICAL ASCENDANCY.

IS SHAPING EVERY PHASE OF

Russian austerity is based on fear of the new media and their power to transform social existence. Russia stands pat on the status quo ante 1850 that produced Marx. There culture ends. The Russian revolution reached the stage of book culture.

Marx never studied or understood causality. He paid no attention to the railway or the steamboat. Russia strives to have a nineteenth century of consumer values but remains a tribal or corporate and non-visual culture.

# expo 67

**for its manifestation
of Gallic levity and
its reversal of the
second law of
thermodynamics
by hotting up the
southern neighbor
by the Canadian**

# COLD FRONT

# BLAST
# BLAST
# BLAST
# BLAST

the Viet Nam war as extravagant
pedagogical effort to
Westernize the East.

# BLESS
# BLESS
# BLESS
# BLESS

Expo 70 in Osaka
as thrifty manoeuvre
to achieve the same end.

# INTER

Now we have landed "where the hand of man never set foot."

# MEDIA

We've had our day at trig and quad and writ our bit as intermidgets.

*Finnegans Wake*

# LOG

One medium of expression modifies another, as one language is changed by contact with another.

Each of our senses is daily modified by the experience of the other senses.

Each medium gives explicitness and stress to one sense over another. Noise weakens touch and taste; sight diminishes the range of the audible, and of taste and smell.

The recent recovery of mime and gesture has revealed the function of the spoken word as the audible translation of an attitude or movement of the mind.

Audible speech split off from gesture and dance as a more explicit codification of interrelations.

# SILENT MASSIVE SCULPTURE

**appeared with the beginning of writing as a fixing of a field of relations intermediate between sight and sound.**

# Is not sculpture the natural predecessor of writing?

# TV is iconic, not pictorial.

# Nudity is sculptural, not visual.

Sculpture is not enclosed by molded space. Writing and architecture are equally enclosed visual space. The visual aspect of space has by then been abstracted from the matrix of all other sensuous apprehensions of space.

Number, said the ancients, is the sounding of space. Geometry is visual space. An enormous effort of collective abstraction precedes the disentangling of these elements from the total matrix of living relations.

Today an even greater energy is needed, first to restore, and then to understand in a connubium, the unity of all the elements which men have abstracted by their codes from the primordial matrix.

Code, language, mechanical medium — all have magical properties which transform, transfigure. But they do not achieve a living spectacle or awareness of the total action required in the electronic age of simultaneities. All the earlier media were exclusive; the electronic age is inclusive.

The more jazz moves away from printed music to improvisation, the closer it comes to speech. Song is slowed-down speech.

# ARRESTED OR FROZEN SPEECH IS *Writing.*

Writing, especially that most abstract kind arising from phonetic alphabet, is an extremely abstract form of technology. The sound and letter elements of such writing have first to be divorced from all meaning. We are beginning this process anew today with the Shannon-type of codification in the Bell laboratories. This time the word itself is the unit to be deprived of meaning for the purposes of codification.

## THE ARTIST HAS ABSOLUTE PITCH FOR HIS TIME.

Forty years earlier Gertrude Stein had performed the same experiment with words in order to recover the underlying gestures which are prior to semantic overlay.

As art ceased to be enmeshed in the texture of ordinary life it became the object of the most intense scrutiny.

Remote folklore, remote societies are being abstracted from their matrix and enlarged by microscopic vision.

Vivisective inspection of all modes of our own inner-outer individual-social lives makes us acutely sensitive to all inter-cultural and inter-media experience.

Each culture, each period has its bias which intensifies, distorts some feature of the total social process. The bias of our culture is precisely to isolate the bias of all others in an effort at orchestration. Social connubium?

The anthropologist is a connoisseur of cultures as art forms.

The student of communications is a connoisseur of media as art forms.

An art form is the manifestation of a huge preference for one mode of experience. Asked what music he liked, Mozart said: "No music." Artists are not consumers.

Communications has emerged as a necessary object of attention in the 20th century, not because it's new, but because it's that portion of the social organism now undergoing elephantiasis.

To reduce this unwieldy growth is going to require great surgical attention and skill.

# Our age is an esthete of the methodologies of all other ages.

THOSE ART GALLERIES
AND MUSEUMS
**which imprison and classify**

BLAST

The Canadian **BEAVER**

apt symbol 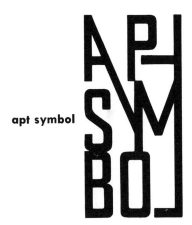 APT SYMBOL

**OF OUR**

**DA**MMED UP CREATIVITY

BLESS
CULTURE SPEAK
as DISLOCation oF MIND
into
MEANING

The adult
never remembers
but the child
never forgets.

The
English can
never remember
and
the Irish can
never
forget.

The
Israelis
can never
remember and
the Arabs can
never forget.

People
never remember
but the computer
never forgets.

the
meeting of
the oral
and written
traditions

**The English can never remember and the Irish can never forget.**

**That observation neatly defines the difference between a society predominantly literary** and one that is mostly oral. And in that cultural cleft have grown some of the greatest careers from Swift and Edmund Burke to Wilde, Shaw, Yeats and Joyce. The same meeting of written and oral traditions occurred in the experience of Dylan Thomas. The ease with which he took to microphone and phonograph was equal only to his joyous storming over his audiences with an eloquence which owed more to the bardic than the literary tradition.

But it is precisely the microphone, phonograph and radio that have readied our perceptions again for enjoyment of poetry as speech and song. In the same way, Bela Balasz showed with respect to film, how it had recovered our sensitivity to the human countenance. The linear, eye-dropper flow of printed words had greatly weakened the plastic power and iconic perception.

In daily affairs, the increase of oral preference and awareness today appears in the new importance of the business-man's lunch as an occasion of serious business. Within the entire business community the shift from paper-work to individual and group brain-storming has taken an oral form.

The executive who has many decisions to make must resort to the speedy oral conference with specially briefed experts. The sheer quantity of information entering into such frequent decisions could not possibly be presented in linear, written form.

In the same way, the panel discussion, the round-table, conferences and conventions, which go on multiplying today, are partly inspired by the radio and public-address system preference for such groupings and partly by speedier means of travel. But they certainly permit the processing and assessing of quantities of information which couldn't be handled by any other means. The lecture is finished in the classroom.

The radio and public-address microphones killed off political oratory. You can't orate into a microphone. You have to chat. And the chat invites the interlocutor and the panel group. In the 1840's in England, G.M. Young tells how statistics (resulting from new communication methods) began to paralyze oratory. And Gladstone was the first speaker to master this new form of expression, as Roosevelt was the first to master the microphone as artillery fixed at the fireside. The home becomes the firing line.

Today the portable tape-recorder is potentially what the kodak was thirty years ago. Witness the great disc by Tony Schwartz *New York 19*. And the tape-recorder has noticeably reshaped the music and folkways worlds as much as the coloured reproduction has altered the worlds of painting and archeology. LP, in conjunction with the tape-recorder, has swiftly extended the boundaries of musical awareness not only to all periods of Western music, but to the music of many other cultures.

Today the teenage music is an environment not something to be played inside an environment.

This is what the book accomplished over centuries with respect to the written word. The LP auditory cultural range is greater than the book, and its operation has been many times quicker. The books speeded up and extended reading habits; but it had the effect also of splitting words and music apart. With the book came silent, solitary reading.

Today our acoustic technology is beginning to restore the ancient union of words and music, but especially the tape recorder has brought back the voice of the bard.

It is not possible to have a very satisfactory look at the centuries of interaction between oral and written culture in a brief space. But to broach the subject at all imposes the need for some retrospect.

To a degree not experienced outside the Anglo-Saxon and English-speaking book belt, even European countries retained their oral tradition after the advent of the printing-press. And now that we have to confront the problems and attitudes of many cultures that have been but slightly touched by lineal, printed communication,

## our opportunities for political ineptitude have greatly increased.

The tendency to underestimate the role of radio in the Near East where the oral tradition is entirely dominant is not unrelated to the Voice of America stress on lineal or talked news in preference to, say, *Porgy and Bess* or the offerings of the G.I. radio that made so many unofficial gains for us.

The illiterate yokel can take over the *Pueblo* as the oral mafia can easily master a literate, legalistic structure by simple by-pass.

For 150 years our poets and artists have been flashing the new oral patterns of culture on the social radar screen. The newspaper of 1800 had already dislodged the book format from its monopoly position in training habits of perception and judgement. After the telegraph this trend was very greatly accelerated.

It is one of the peculiar biases of book format that it makes its users oblivious of the fact that it is a highly specialized form of technology; and they readily assume that all other media are also gimmicks for conveying information, because they assume that is also the role of the book. It is easy to see how readers of print got into this state of mind, since the book is archetypally a mechanical gimmick. It is not so easy to get these readers to see that the use of print creates modes of thought and space that are quite alien to other cultures, and even alien to our own earlier culture. It is very hard to get a man in the print belt of culture to recognize that the *form* of print is itself cultural and deeply biased. The fish knows nothing of water.

**But in the Western world, our more recent technology has not just dislodged the book form as a gimmick. It has brought us back to oral and acoustic culture by many indirect paths, as well.**

In the 19th century, Poland, Russia, and the Balkans got the latest newspaper technology before they had been exposed for very long to the book. In the 17th century, America got the latest European technology (the book) minus all the other forms of culture. The pattern of assembly-line production from movable type had no rivals in forming American habits of perception.

# The Ford plant in Detroit was a late by-product of the Gutenberg plant. The assembly line is liquidated by the computer. The prayer mat will succeed the Cadillac.

The revolutionary impact of the newspaper format in Middle Europe and Russia was unmediated by the centuries of book skills we had acquired. The daily snapshotting of the whole of society, or of the globe, which is the press format, creates a mode of group awareness quite alien to the individualism of the isolated book-reader.

WHAT IS TO
BE THE POL
ITICAL AND
ITICAL AND
SOCIAL IMP
ACT OF RAD
IO AND TV
TECHNOLO
GY ON PEOP
LES WHO HA
VE HAD NEI
THER BOOK
NOR PRESS?

**To the person of book culture, habituated to think of the book as a neutral environment serving his independent mind, it is heresy to say that the impact of these forms is quite separate from anything they happen to be used to say or express. But it is only necessary to notice the patterns of learning and association before print or before writing to discover that the message or information conveyed by the supposedly neutral medium is not the major component of such situations.**

It is all the easier today to observe such matters when the effect of technology since the telegraph has been to recreate the conditions of simultaneity which characterize pre-literate cultures. The obsession of poets since Wordsworth with the spoken word as primary esthetic datum, is as central to our new culture as non-Euclidean geometry. The current congeniality between primeval and sophisticated attitudes was not a foreseen consequence of an ever-improved mastery over the material world. But neither were the consequences of writing itself foreseen.

## IN A
## PRE-LITERATE WORLD
## WORDS ARE NOT SIGNS.

They evoke things directly in what
psychologists call acoustic space.
By being named, the thing is simply
there. Acoustic space is a dynamic
or harmonic field. It exists while
the music or sound persists. And
the hearer is one with it, as with
music. Acoustic space is the space-
world of primeval man. Even his
visual experience is much
subordinate to his auditory and
magical domain wherein there
is neither centre nor margin
nor point of view.

**The pre-literate artist knows no vertical or
horizontal axes. He does not enclose space but
models it in all dimensions simultaneously,
even when drawing or painting. There is no
upside down in native art.**

**In this respect, sculpture stands mid-way
between the auditory primeval world and
the visual world of literate man.**

The step of translating the auditory into the visual which occurred with phonetic writing did not happen quickly. But it was a most radical step. To abstract sound from meaning and then to enclose that sound in a visual space happened only with the Greek alphabet. The Phoenicians proceeded only so far as to visualize consonantal sounds. And this abstraction achieved by the Greeks and transferred to the Romans created an imperial visual net in which the Western world has captured every oral culture that it has met. No other kind of writing attempted this abstraction. And no other kind of writing had the resulting means of control over other cultures. Only phonetic writing creates the habit of matching, of realistic representation.

**Not until the PHOTOGRAPH MOVIE and TV did there appear any rival to the insatiable cultural conquest of the phonetic alphabet.**

So far as the alphabet affected our own culture we have the repudiation of it by Plato in the *Phaedrus* and in his epistles, on the ground that it arrests the act of thought in a way fatal to the creative function:

*This discovery of yours will create forgetfulness in the learners' souls, because they will not use their memories; they will trust to the external written characters and not remember of themselves ... they will be tiresome company having the show of wisdom without the reality.*

Contrary to popular superstition it is the oral tradition which ensures fixity. Robert Redfield in *The Primitive World and its Transformations* points to the timeless character of pre-literate societies where exclusively oral communication makes for intimacy and homogeneity of experience. It is the advent of writing that sets into motion the urban revolution. With TV we enter once more the heliotropic noughttime (Joyce).

With phonetic writing, the visual enclosure of acoustic space, there occurs the arrest of the flux of thought that permits analysis. Almost at once there were discovered all the boundaries between the verbal and physical arts and sciences which have been traditional to our own time. The breaking of the acoustic space barrier created many walls between the modes of knowledge such as are tending to dissolve once more in our own time. The dynamics of the technology of phonetic writing set in motion a series of spectacular changes which have been superseded only by their resolution in the technology of writing by means of light itself in television.

The initial abstraction of sight (phonetic alphabet) from sound so upset the equilibrium of oral cultures that henceforth they existed only in the mode of rapid change. Yet all cultures strive to return to the integral inclusiveness of the oral state. For it is only in such intimacy and completeness of interpersonal awareness that balance seems possible.

In Western history it is the period when a brief balance between written and oral experience emerges for a few decades that we mark as the great cultural flowerings. Today we are approaching the means of initiating and prolonging such conditions. But our past is a record of the brief moments when one particular art seemed to approach the oral ideal of an inclusive consciousness: architecture in the 12th century, drama and painting in the 16th, music in the 19th.

Today the return to oral conditions of communication is not merely to be noted in the strictly acoustic sphere. The oral is the world of the non-linear, of all-at-onceness and ESP. There are no lines or directions in acoustic space, but rather a simultaneous field. It is non-Euclidean. And the newspaper in setting up a dozen book pages on one page was already a big step towards this sort of cultural simultaneity and non-lineality. The telegraph extended simultaneity to the globe, creating diplomacy without walls.

The external landscape techniques of the Romantic poets and painters were pushed to the extreme point where they suddenly become internal and musical with Rimbaud and the symbolists. Instead of using a single external space to evoke and control mental states, it was suddenly discovered that many spaces and many times could be included in a single poem or picture. The newspaper contributed directly to this new art form. And no sooner had this occurred than artists were enabled to see that all language and experience was, and had always been, this simultaneous and many-layered thing.

**ALL OF THE**

# NEW MEDIA

**HAVE ENRICHED
OUR PERCEPTIONS OF**

**AND**

**OLDER MEDIA**

**THEY ARE TO THE MAN-
MADE ENVIRONMENT WHAT
SPECIES ARE TO BIOLOGY.**

# PROBES OR EXPERIMENTS

It is easy now to see that language has always been a mass medium even as the new media are new languages having each its own unique grammar and esthetic modes.

FOR
ENCLOSING
TERRESTRIAL

## NATURE

IN A

# MAN-
# MADE
# ENVIRON-
# MENT

that transfers the
evolutionary process
from biology to
technology.

# THE
# PEOPLE

i tui sicut piscine i esebon: q sut
a filie mltitudinis: Nasus tu
turris libani: q respicit cotra
ic. Caput tuum ut carmelus:
capilli tui sicut purpura regis
analibz: Quam pulcra es· et
a carissima in delicijs. Statu
simulata est palme: et ubera
cis. Dixi. Ascendam in palmam:
nda fruct9 eius: Et erut ubera
t botri vince: et odor oris tui
or malor: guttur tuu sicut vi
ntimu: Dignu dilecto meo ad
u: labijsq3 et dentibz illius ad
ndu. Ego dilecto meo: et ad
tio ei9. Veni dilecte mi egredi
t agru: comoremur in villis.
urgam9 ad vineas: videam9
vinea· si floret frut9: si parturi
oruerunt malapunica: Ibi
i ubera mea:
re i portis nris: Dilecte mi
vetera dilecte mi seruaui abi·
s michi det te fratrem C uni
tu sugente ubera matris mee:
ia te foris et deosculet et iam
o despiciat? Apphendam te et
mu matris mee: et i cubiculu
s mee: Ibi me docebis: 7 dabo
idu ex vino codito: et mustu
ranator meor. Leua ei9 sub
eo: et dextera illi9 amplexabit
iuro vos filie iherlm: ne suscit
t uigilare faciatis dilecta: do
lit. Que est ista que ascendit
i delicijs· affluens: innixa sup
u? Sub arbore malo suscit

Greeting the Caedmon record album of Dylan Thomas reading "Under Milkwood", Harvey Breit says:

# 'UNDER MILKWOOD' IS A CELLO CONCERTO

"Whatever it is, whatever else it is, 'Under Milkwood' is a cello concerto — if you substitute Dylan's voice for Casals' cello. The solo passages are lovingly modulated, ranging from pastoral glissando to bawdy fortissimo . . . . The freedom of the form was just right for Dylan, for his imagination and rhetoric, and conceivably he could have gone on and given us a series of such concerti, on love, on politics, on poetry itself."

The careers of Yeats and Joyce were even more deeply involved in the qualities of the spoken word as they met the literary tradition. And all three of these men were very conscious of the 20th century advantages of having their cultural roots in a pre-literate world. That which in them might appear as mere romantic preference can, however, be set in a perspective of advancing or unfolding technology.

**Frank O'Connor highlights
a basic distinction between
oral and written traditions:**

"By the hokies, there was a man in this one time
by name of Ned Sullivan, and he had a queer thing
happen to him late one night and he coming up the
Valley Road from Durlas."

That is how a folk story begins, or should begin,
and woe betide the story-teller whoever he may be
who forgets his story is first and foremost NEWS,
that there is a listener he must grip by the lapel and
shout at if necessary till he has attracted his attention. Yet that is how no printed story should begin,
because such a story seems tame when you remove
it from its warm nest by the cottage fire, from the
sense of an audience with its interjections, and the
feeling of terror at what may lurk in the darkness
outside. This is a tale, and even when handled by a
master like Kipling, it looks and is contrived.

Printing from movable type is, perhaps, the first instance of the mechanization of a handicraft. It was a 15th century achievement which was the meeting point of a wide range of skills. Printing from fixed type or blocks had been common in China centuries before, and in Europe, too, decades before Gutenberg. But movable type was a different matter. It can even be viewed as a sort of assembly-line situation by which manuscript yields to mass production. And this latest form of European technology was one of the first items to come to America. So far as social effect was concerned, the arrival of the printing press and the book on the scene devoid of any other established communication arts was decisive. The parallel might be found in the arrival of the newspaper in Poland before the book.

**IN THIS CENTURY THE LATEST TECHNOLOGY (MOVIES, RADIO, TV) HAS ARRIVED IN SOME COUNTRIES BEFORE THE BOOK OR NEWSPAPER. TO THE ORIENTAL THE X-RAY QUALITY OF TV (THE INNER-TRIPPINESS) IS INTENSIFYING THEIR ORIENTAL INWARD- NESS AT THE SAME TIME THAT THEY WESTERNIZE IN A NINETEENTH-CENTURY PATTERN. THE CONFLICT OF THESE FORMS IS EXTREMELY TRAUMATIC AS IT IS FOR OUR TEENAGERS.**

For reasons which are hard to discover, there does not exist any body of observation about the impact of various media of communication on pre-existing cultural patterns.

# WHAT DOES THE ADVENT OF LITERACY DO TO THE PSYCHOLOGICAL AND SOCIAL STRUCTURE OF A CULTURE?

To answer that, one must analyze and observe the operation of translating sound into sight. Before this operation, words have a very different status. In native societies words are not signs referring from one situation to another. Before writing it is natural and inevitable to regard words as "magical" powers which directly evoke a thing. In the past century poets and artists have recovered this view of language. It is a view which since Baudelaire has deeply modified the literary view of language.

Familiarity with pre-literate cultures has revealed many aspects of our literary language which had long been hidden by the unconscious bias of writing and print.

The translation of the oral into the visual, with a *fixed* point of view, constitutes an arrest of the auditory flux which permits analysis of language and enumeration and classification of all the mental modes which it incorporates. But it also sets up an oscillation in the reader's mind caused by the continuous act of translation from sound to sight and sight to sound, which is the act of reading.

The peculiarity of the Phoenician and Greek alphabet must be studied if we are to grasp the dynamics of Western culture. So far as I know, this˙ phonetic alphabet is unlike any other. It alone is based on the abstraction of the sound of words from the meaning of words.

By way of approaching the printed book it may serve to point out that to read a manuscript roll or codex is so laborious and slow a process that it was only natural to such readers to memorize all that they read. To return to consult such materials was extremely inconvenient. So, both the ancient and medieval worlds having their reading on the tip of their tongues, preferred oratorical and disputational modes of teaching and expression. That meant learning in groups.

With the printed book individual study became possible. But above all, speed of reading enabled the individual like a Tamburlaine or Dr. Faustus to cover authors and subjects in a few weeks which had in manuscript conditions occupied a lifetime. On the other hand, the reader ceased to memorize. The book became a work of reference. The oral tradition folded fairly soon. But in the Elizabethan drama there was a brief meeting of the old oral culture and the new literary culture.

Manuscript culture had fostered encyclopedism as a convenience when reading was slow and books were scarce. Printing fostered specialism, classified data and antiquarianism. It fostered nationalism and vernaculars, since the international Latin did not offer sufficient scope for markets to the printers. Print split apart words and music; but printed scores made possible the elaborate instrumentation of seventeenth- and eighteenth-century music. Print diminished sensitivity in the plastic arts, in painting and architecture, but created new dimensions of urban space. The very linear and rectilinear layout of words on the printed page transformed the nature of spelling, grammar and prose style. And a society like America relying, as it did at first, almost entirely on printed information and art, naturally developed a great sensitivity to the technology of print and its basic mass-production principle.

America, being at first almost solely a book culture, did little to develop the other arts. So that even today there is in America as there is in no other part of the world, the assumption that culture means book culture. This view makes it difficult for us to see baseball or popular music as culture. It makes it difficult for us to see the newspaper as a unique art form. It has meant that we are the last to study the grammar of film or the language of architecture.

**Our obsession with the book as the archetype of culture has not even encouraged us to consider the book itself as a peculiar and arty way of packaging experience.**

But until the book is seen as a very specialized form of art and technology we cannot today get our bearings among the new arts and the new media.

It was the newspaper that by 1800 presented the greatest challenge to the book. The book met the challenge by assimilation. The novels of Scott and Dickens, the poetry of Byron wrapped up the great new world-panoramas of the power-press in new fictional techniques of landscape and vignette. For the book page as such has none of the mosaic scope of the newspaper page. With the telegraph there came the dimension of simultaneity to be added to the newspaper's inclusive social image. To this new challenge came the mosaic response of Rimbaud's *Illuminations,* of Mallarme's *Un Coup de Dés,* of *Ulysses* and *The Waste Land.*

If printing was the mechanization of writing, the telegraph was the electrification of writing. If the movie was the mechanization of movement and gesture, TV is the electronification of the same. Each of these steps in making more explicit an earlier technology modifies all other media. The newspaper changed poetic technique, the movie modified the novel, and TV changed the movie. The telegraph gave us diplomacy without walls as the motorcar gave us the home without walls. But perhaps all these matters and many more can be enclosed in the consideration of how the telephone is not a neutral channel or convenience but a form which, rooted in our entire technology, has also transformed interpersonal life and the entire structure of business and politics.

With the electric codification of information came the cryptogram and the present age of cryptoanalysis. Hence the national trauma of the *Pueblo*.

**BLESS**

the fast talking

ILLITERATE

AMERICAN

for his

FACE to FACE to EAR to EAR

methods of

LEARNING

**THE COMMUNIST MANIFESTO**

**REAR VIEW MIRROR**

OF A

**FÊTE ACC⊏**
**FATE ACCOM⊓**
**FAIT ACCOMPL⊓**

BLESS

BLESS

# FINNEGANS WAKE

## REAR END LOOK?
## EAR BEGIN LOOK?
# RIRE END LOOK

at the information
environment of
tribal communism.

# IT WOULD BE A MISTAKE TO SUPPOSE THAT THE TREND OF CULTURE TOWARD THE ORAL AND ACOUSTIC MEANS THAT THE BOOK IS BECOMING

It means rather that the book, as it loses its monopoly as a cultural form will acquire new roles. Nobody seems to know much about why the paper-back flopped in the 30's and succeeded in the 50's. But it is a fact which probably has some relation to TV, on one hand, and to LP, on the other.

OBSOLETE.

The TV screen is close in form and immediacy to the book page. The movie screen was not. TV puts walls around the home again and the movie does not. Based on the flexibility of the tape-recorder, LP has knocked out the walls between all the periods of music and brought the folkways and folk music of all cultures into accessible form. In these respects, it transcends the flexibility of the book in some ways. But it has brought authors and poets into a new relation with readers, reinforcing the interest of the book.

# PRINT WOULD SEEM TO HAVE LOST MUCH OF ITS MONOPOLY AS A CHANNEL OF INFORMATION, BUT IT HAS ACQUIRED NEW INTEREST AS A TOOL IN THE TRAINING OF PERCEPTION.

This perhaps appears in the new criticism which is so unsympathetic to many of those trained in an earlier period of book culture. As a tool in the training of perception, the book, I think, has acquired a great new role in the past two decades. The unexplained popularity of highbrow paperbacks may be related to this complex situation.

It is not strange that the young should respond untaught to rock-and-roll as an interpretation of their world of accelerated stress and change. Or that business men should abandon much of their former paperwork for the quick briefing by experts or the making of deals at lunch. The roundtable, the frequent conferences and group-brainstorming are as much a part of our situation today as the factors which shaped up the first TV election. Today we are in the midst of our first TV war. The public participation is total.

As the most completely book-minded people in the world, North Americans would seem to be moving swiftly into new orbits of experience for which their bookishness has not entirely prepared them. Perhaps the best strategy of culture is to size up the book and the printed word in their widest relations and to decide from there. Our book technology has Gutenberg at one end and the Ford assembly lines at the other. Both are obsolete.

FEEDING
LANGUAGE
AND
THOUGHT

?

THROUGH  THE  TYPEWRITER

日本人が　暗号文を　開発しようとしたとき

日本語の漢字は　記号で表すには　あまりに

総括的で　過ぎないのに気づいた。

そこで、彼らは　いわゆる「タイプライター　アルハベット

と呼んでいる　記号（文字）に頼ったのである。

When the Japanese sought to develop a cryptogram they discovered that their written character was too inclusive for code. They resorted to what they called the "Typewriter Alphabet."

Quand les Japonais ont essayé de développer un cryptogramme, ils ont découvert que leurs caractères avaient une signification trop complexe pour être mis en langage codé. Ils ont recouru à ce qu'ils ont appelé "L'alphabet en vedette."

Когда японцы пытались изобрести шифр (криптограмму), то они убедились, что их письменные знаки, благодаря своему содержательному объему, не поддавались кодифицированию. Они прибегнули к тому, что они назвали "дактилографическим алфавитом".

Typing reduced expression from art to craft, from personal to impersonal. It's a means of transcribing thought, not expressing it. It relieves the expression of thought of personal quirks and picturesque speech by its immediate and glaring clarity--never confused by the swirls and illegibility of handwriting. It can lead to greater comprehension-apprehension.

Typing is a helpful discipline. Tortuous phrases disappear under a dazzle of keys. Circumlocution seems impossible because the mechanical act of putting words on

paper is a means to an end--the way to
the point. Thoughts transposed into type
are in effect published, and publication
removes the expression of those thoughts
from the intimate and personal sphere.
Publication is a self-invasion of privacy.

Handwriting is now obsolete, resorted
to for inconsequential matters, memos,
lecture notes, telephone numbers and
personal letters. Diaries and involved
personal letters are no longer in style.

As a writing machine, the typewriter
is far more efficient than the hand.
Your fingers type automatically and
simultaneously what you're thinking.
When you handwrite, you write carefully
and slowly, and usually less colloquially.

The typewriter is a good distancer. You're less closely attached to what you're writing. Handwriting remains part of you.

It's difficult to see the shape of sentences in the maze of handwriting. When typing, you're more conscious of the appearance of your writing. You view it stretched out before you, detached from you. The rhythm of typing favours short, concise sentences, sentences with oral form. The typewriter makes you more conscious of the acoustic qualities of words, since the words themselves are produced in a background of sound. There's a tendency to say words to the typewriter--some business schools teach the sounding of words while typing as the most efficient practise.

(Justice Charles E. Wyzanski, Jr.)

Brandeis had one curiously expensive habit. In preparing an opinion as a Justice of the Court he regularly sent many rough drafts to the Court Printer, and then worked from galleys as other lawyers would work from typewritten drafts. Sometimes, as in his celebrated dissent in the O'Fallon case, he dispatched perhaps more than a score of versions of his opinion to the printer's shop on Twelfth Street before he was satisfied with the product. A reason for this extraordinary use of printed rather than typewritten copies may have been that only when a document appeared to him as he thought it would appear to a reader was he able to judge its quality. But whatever the reason, the result was as striking stylistically as it was substantively.

(Robert Lincoln O'Brien, 1904)

The invention of the typewriter has given a tremendous impetus to the dictating habit. This means not only greater diffuseness, inevitable with any lessening of the tax on words which the labour of writing imposes, but also brings forward the point of view of the one who speaks. There is the disposition on the part of the speaker to explain, as if watching the facial expressions of his hearers to see how far they are following. This attitude is not lost when his audience becomes merely a clicking typewriter. It is no uncommon thing in the typewriting booths at the Capitol in Washington to see Congressmen in dictating letters use the most vigorous gestures as if the oratorical methods of persuasion could be transmitted to the printed page.

(*The Wonderful Writing Machine* by Bruce Bliven, Jr.)

Some of the influences of the typewriter on English composition were all to the good. Teachers had noticed, early in the game, that the clarity of machine writing forced people to improve their spelling and punctuation.

105

The penman, in doubt about whether the "i" should precede the "e", had usually written an ambiguous "ie" that could be taken for "ei". Or had made the entire word a snakelike ripple that could be understood only from context.

Typewriting brought things out into the open. Dictionary sales zoomed, and persons who had never before given the semicolon any serious thought began to use it on the slightest excuse. There were those wretches who, confronted by the "e" and "i" dilemma, resorted to the low dodge of typing "e", backspacing, and then hitting the "i" on top of it. But, for the most part, good typists were good at spelling and skillful in the use of punctuation, if only because it saved erasing.

(*Henry James at Work* by Theodora Bosanquet)

The practice of dictation was begun in the nineties. By 1907 it was a confirmed habit, its effects being easily recognizable in his style, which became more and more like free, involved, unanswered talk. "I know", he said once to me, "that I'm too diffuse when I'm dictating." But he found dictation not only an easier but a more inspiring method of composing than writing with his own hand, and he considered that the gain in expression more than compensated for any loss of concision. The spelling out of words, the indication of the commas, were scarcely felt as a drag on the movement of his thought. "It all seems," he once explained, "to be so much more effectively and unceasingly *pulled* out of me in speech than in writing." Indeed, at the time when I began to work for him, he had reached the stage at which the click of a Remington machine acted as a positive spur.

. . . it was almost impossibly disconcerting to speak to something that made no responsive sound at all. Once or twice when he was ill and in bed I took down a note or two by hand, but as a rule he liked to have the typewriter moved into his bedroom for even the shortest letters. Yet there were to the end certain kinds of work which he was obliged to do with a pen. Plays, if they were to be kept within the limits of possible performance, and short stories, if they were to remain within the bounds of publication in a monthly magazine, must be written by hand. He was well aware that the manual labour of writing was his best aid to a deserved brevity. The plays—such as *The Outcry*, for instance—were copied straight from his manuscript, since he was too much afraid of 'the murderous limits of the English theatre' to risk the temptation of dictation and embroidery. With the short stories he allowed himself a little more freedom, dictating them from his written draft and expanding them as he went to an extent which inevitably defeated his original purpose. It is almost literally true to say of the sheaf of tales collected in *The Finer Grain* that they were all written in response to a single request for a short story for *Harper's Monthly Magazine*. The length was to be about 5,000 words and each promising idea was cultivated in the optimistic belief that it would produce a flower too frail and small to demand any exhaustive treatment. But even under pressure of being written by hand, with dictated interpolations rigidly restricted, each in turn pushed out to lengths that no chopping could reduce to the word limit. The tale eventually printed was *Crapy Cornelia,* but, although it was the shortest of the batch, it was thought too long to be published in one number and appeared in two sections, to the great annoyance of the author.

Attentive readers of the novels may perhaps find the distinction between these two groups less remarkable than it seems to their writer. They may even wonder whether the second marriage was not rather a silver wedding, with the old romantic mistress cleverly disguised as a woman of the world. The different note was possibly due more to the substitution of dictation for pen and ink than to any profound change of heart. But whatever the reason, their author certainly found it necessary to spend a good deal of time working on earlier tales before he considered them fit for appearance in the company of those composed later.

. . . he "broke ground", as he said, by talking to himself day by day about the characters and construction until the persons and their actions were vividly present to his inward eye. This soliloquy was of course recorded on the typewriter. He had from far back tended to dramatize all the material that life gave him, and he more and more prefigured his novels as staged performances, arranged in acts and scenes, with characters making their observed entrances and exits. These scenes he worked out until he felt himself so thoroughly possessed of the action that he could begin on the dictation of the book itself — a process which has been incorrectly described by one critic as re-dictation from a rough draft. It was nothing of the kind.

The preliminary sketch was seldom consulted after the novel began to take permanent shape, but the same method of "talking out" was resorted to at difficult points of the narrative as it progressed, always for the sake of testing in advance the values of the persons involved in a given situation, so that their creator should ensure their right action both for the development of the drama and the truth of their relations to each other. The knowledge of all the conscious motives and concealments of his creatures, gained by unwearied observation of their attitudes behind the scenes, enabled Henry James to exhibit them with a final confidence that dispensed with explanations. Among certain stumbling blocks in the path of the perfect comprehension of his readers is their uneasy doubt of the sincerity of the conversational encounters recorded. Most novelists provide some clue to help their readers to distinguish truth from falsehood, and in the theatre, although husbands and wives may be deceived by lies, the audience is usually privy to the plot. But a study of the Notes to *The Ivory Tower* will make it clear that between the people created by Henry James lying is as frequent as among mortals and not any easier to detect.

In *Museum Without Walls,* André Malraux faces up to the modern situation with respect to the art of painting. He asks us to consider the effect on painters of having before them the art of many other painters. Less than a century ago the painter tended to be acquainted with a very limited range of paintings. He would have had to travel to many places to see any appreciable number of paintings by one painter. His ideas of the work of a whole period were necessarily of the sketchiest. Today the reproduction of the art of men and periods is such as to permit the detailed knowledge of the styles and techniques of all periods of Western painting. In addition we know the painting, sculpture and architecture of dozens of other cultures in far greater detail than we once knew the art of our own time.

The "genuine fake" is often as expensive as the original. Corot said: "I have painted 2,000 pictures; 5,000 of them are in the U.S.A."

Quite recently, we have all experienced a parallel occurrence in the world of music. LP records have done for music what Skira did for painting. Whereas we had been accustomed to a very limited orchestral repertory — a few composers and only a few of their works — LP suddenly opened up the music horizons to include the music of many centuries, many cultures. The Folkways series brings us the song and dance of the world. For the composer this means that he writes now for an audience altogether different in its experience. His own experience has also been profoundly modified. He can no longer accept nor expect others to accept a dominant musical style, fashion, convention. Our music now includes the music of many periods and cultures in a vital and living relationship. And this had never occurred before in the world since there were no means of making a present which included so much and excluded so little. The same situation exists in poetry. There have been great periods of poetry which grew from the discovery of other kinds of poetry which could be translated and adapted in order to develop new forms of experience in one region or country. It could be argued that great periods are always periods of translation. In the Elizabethan time English was enlarged and enriched by a large influx of foreign styles. Printing made available, suddenly, to a large audience, the styles of many Greek and Latin poets who were swiftly adapted to the resources of English. Older English poetry was available as well as French, Spanish and Italian styles. All of these got onto the popular stage in various modes and degrees. Twentieth century poetry has absorbed the styles of Irish and Welsh bards, of Japanese and Chinese, of many native cultures. Earlier, the Romantic poets had very consciously gone to the old ballads and to popular folklore in a search for new effects and new experiences which would release the human spirit from the chains of conventional perception. The discovery of rural landscape and of natural scenery, they felt, was a principal means of leading the spirit in the paths of self-discovery and meditation. Towards these ends they incorporated, not only the old ballads and verbal incantation, but the art of painting as well. From Gray's *Elegy in a Country Churchyard* to Blake's *Tyger* or from Blake to Scott, Wordsworth and Byron, poets were avid technicians of picturesque painting styles using the external scene to flash upon the inward eye precious knowledge of the symphony of nature. They used the external scene to distinguish and to explore the wide range of passions and feelings, and to discover new mental states. To arrest and fix these fleeting states by means of carefully delineated scenes was their aim and ambition.

By the time of Baudelaire and Rimbaud the use of painting as a means of fixing a mental state (always starting with the effect to be produced) had been pushed a very long way. Suddenly the visual boundaries yielded to music; the symbolist poets discovered the acoustic space of auditory imagination. This breakthrough from the visual world into the acoustic world was the most revolutionary thing that has occured in Western culture since the invention of phonetic writing. To understand the human, social and artistic bearings of this event is indispensible today whether for the teacher or the citizen. Most of the cultural confusion of our world results from this huge shift in the geography of perception and feeling.

The artistic developments, which we associate with the romantics in painting and poetry, had consisted in the impressionistic use of external landscape as a means of exploring and defining mental states. When these artists came to the frontiers of visual landscape they passed over into its opposite, as it were, namely, acoustic or auditory space. This unexpected reversal or translation of the visual into the acoustic happened when the silent movies became sound pictures, and again when radio was suddenly metamorphosed into TV. And the consequences of these shifts between sight and sound need to be understood by the teacher today since they turn the language of the arts into a jabberwocky that has to be unscrambled to be understood. When the arts shifted from sight to sound, from visual to acoustic organization of experience, the tempo and rhythm of our culture shifted as though an LP disc were suddenly shifted to 78 r.p.m.

Today it's easy to know what the effect of writing was on culture because we have detailed knowledge of many cultures that have no writing. We have also watched them undergoing the impact of writing and print. Pre-literate man has no experience of vertical or horizontal planes in visual perception. He doesn't use his eyes in the same way as a literate man. He doesn't recognize the contents of photographs until instructed. A movie to him is not a picture at all, but a blur. He lives in an auditory world, a verbal universe. For him, words are not signs or symbols. They don't refer to something. They are the thing itself. We understand this easier in relation to music. We know that music need not refer to something. A phrase or melody defines itself and evokes an attitude or a state of mind instantly. But the phrase or meldoy does not refer to such attitude or state. It's the state and we're the music. This is the preliterate attitude to language. The word "tree" is tree, because it has the power to evoke tree. Acoustically but not semantically considered, a word is a complex set of harmonic relations as beautiful as a seashell. These relations are dynamic. They are simultaneous, set off by silence. The set of harmonic relations constitutes a field entity which experimental psychologists refer to as acoustic space. If visual space is greatly dependent on our habits of seeing, acoustic space is entirely structured by our hearing. Psychologists tell us that acoustic space is spherical because we hear simultaneously from all directions. It has no lines or directions. It contains nothing; it's contained in nothing. It has no horizons or boundary lines. All its relations are simultaneous; it's a physical entity defined by these dynamic relations.

The newspaper page upset book culture and the book page profoundly. The Romantic poets took courage from this upset to revolt against book culture. The format of the book page offers a linear, not a picturesque perspective. It fosters a single tone and attitude between a writer, reader, subject, whereas the newspaper breaks up this lineality and singleness of tone and perspective, offering many book pages at the same moment. The telegraph gave instantaneity to this picturesque news landscape, turned the news-sheet into a global photograph or world snapshot.

The press became a daily experience of all the cultures of the globe. It became a space-time landscape of many times, many places, given as single experience. With the arrival of photography this verbal landscape shifted to a pictorial one. With radio it became verbal again, but not the printed word. With TV it becomes both. But by 1870 when Rimbaud made his verbal landscapes (which he called illuminations or colored plates) the newspaper format had revolutionized poetry. Nobody so far as I know has commented on the relation of Richard Wagner to the newspaper, but his esthetic program for including the whole of the human mythic past in a simultaneous musical present doesn't need much explaining. Electricity, in the same way, creates musical politics.

The difficulty which most people experience with the poetry of Rimbaud, Mallarmé, Eliot, Joyce, or the difficulty they imagine to be present in the work of Picasso or abstract art, is exactly the difficulty a listener might have in trying to listen to a disc played at the wrong speed. Any newspaper page, since the telegraph, is a symbolist mosaic.

Here's Rimbaud's *Dimanche* or *Sunday:*

When homework is done, the inevitable descent from heaven and the visitation of memories and the session of rhythms invade the dwelling, the head and the world of the spirit.

A horse scampers off along the suburban turf and the gardens and the wood lots, besieged by the carbonic plague. Somewhere in the world a wretched melodramatic woman is sighing for unlikely desertions. Desperadoes are languishing for storms, drunkenness, wounds. Little children are stifling curses along the rivers.

I must study some more to the sound of the consuming work which forms in all the people and rises up in them.

The organization of experience here is acoustic and iconic rather than visual. Yet the various units of experience are visualized. There is a landscape, but it includes more than one space in its space and more than one time in its time. It's a simultaneous order such as music readily offers. A merely visual landscape, however, can offer only one space at one time:

> *Behold her single in the field*
> *Yon solitary Highland lass*
> *Reaping and singing by herself*
> *Stop here or gently pass*

The sort of landscape which Rimbaud presents is a kind of interior landscape of the mind. But it also began to be common in the newspaper fifty years before poets took it over.

The more that one says about acoustic space the more one realizes that it's the thing that mathematicians and physicists of the past fifty years have been calling space-time, relativity, and non-Euclidean systems of geometry. And it was into this acoustic world that the poets and painters began to thrust in the mid-19th century. Like Coleridge's Mariner, they were the first that ever burst into that silent sea. This was the world of experience emerging to Keats when he spoke of "magic casements opening on the foam of perilous seas in faerie lands forlorn." It was to be a world in which the eye listens, the ear sees, and in which all the senses assist each other in concert.

From one point of view, words themselves are a kind of symphony of the sensorium, a cinematic flow which includes all of our "five and country senses." Writing meant a translation of this many-layered concert into the sense of sight alone. Reading and writing in this respect represent an intense degree of specialization of experience. Writing meant that the acoustic world with its magic power over the being of things was arrested and banished to a humble sphere. Writing meant the power of fixing the flux of words and of thought. Writing permitted analysis of thought-processes which gave rise to the categories of knowledge. With writing came the power of visually enclosing not only acoustic space but architectural space. With writing came the separation of music from the dance, of both from words. Before writing, all these division were merged in a single "mythic" knowledge, a single rhythm where there was no present but all was now. *Four Quartets* of T. S. Eliot is a complete guide to our own recovery of acoustic modes of knowing our own and past experience. *Finnegans Wake* of James Joyce is a verbal universe in which press, movie, radio, TV merge with the languages of the world to form a Feenichts Playhouse of metamorphoses.

Modern technology which began by a visual recovery of the past in print has now come to the point of acoustic and visual recovery which installs us once more in the heart of primeval consciousness and experience. If the Romantics pushed at the walls of vision until they yielded and became a shell of sound, we have all of us pounded on the doors of perception until they admitted us to a world which is both and end and a beginning. In our time we are reliving at high speed the whole of the human past. As in a speeded-up film, we are traversing all ages, all experience, including the experience of prehistoric man. Our experience is not exclusive of other people's experience but inclusive — symphonic and orchestral, rather than linear or melodic. This gigantic flashback may sound like a collective version of that movie of a man's past life that is said to flash on when he is drowning. We may be drowning. But if so, the flood of experience in which we are drowning is very much a part of the culture we have created. The flood is not something outside our culture. It is a self-invasion of privacy. And so it's not catastrophic. We can turn it off if we choose, if we wake up to the fact that the faucets of change are inside the ark of society, not outside.

# Media are artificial extensions of sensory existence.

each an externalized species of the inner genus sensation. The cultural environment created by externalization of modes of sensation now favours the predominance of one sense or another. These species struggle through mutations in a desperate attempt at adaptation and survival.

Accidents foster an uneven rate of development of communication facilities. Circumstances fostering in one age painting, sculpture, music, may produce a bulwark against the effects of, say, printing. But the same bulwark may be quite useless before the impact of movies or TV.

Improvements in the means of communication are based on a shift from one sense to another. This involves a rapid refocusing of all previous experience. Any change in the means of communication produces a chain of revolutionary consequences at every level of culture and politics. Because of the complexity of this process, prediction and control are impossible.

John Donne and George Herbert transferred to the new printed page of the 17th century many effects which had previously been popular in the pictorial world of the later Middle Ages. For them print had made the visual arts recessive and quaint. In this century the sudden predominance of the graphic arts has made print recessive. We filter one past culture through the screen of others and of our own—a game we play with whole cultures and epochs as easily as we could previously combine phrases from two languages.

With writing comes inner speech, the dialogue with one-self—a result of translating the verbal into the visual (writing) and translating the visual into the verbal (reading)—a complex process for which we pay a heavy psychic and social price—the price, as James Joyce puts it, of ABCED-minded-ness. Literate man experiences an inner psychic withdrawal from his external senses which gives him a heavy psychic and social limp. But the rewards are very rich.

Today we experience in reverse, what pre-literate man faced with the advent of writing. Today we are, in a technical if not literary sense, post-literate. Literacy: a brief phase.

Aristotle described speech as the arrest of the flowing of thought. Today speech begins to look like an obsolete technology. The sounds we utter are structured in acoustic space by noise spaced in silence. What silence is to acoustic space, darkness is to visual space. Speech structures interpersonal distances. These distances aren't just physical, but emotional and cultural. We involuntarily raise our voices when speaking to those who don't understand our language. Entering a silent house, we call a name in a tone intended to extend throughout that space.

Words are an orchestral harmony of touch, taste, sight, sound. Writing is the abstraction of the visual from this complex. With writing comes power: command over space.

Manuscript culture, based on parchment and the scarcity of writing materials, made for a high degree of memorization—the inevitable result of the scarcity of manuscripts, the slowness of reading them and the difficulty of referring to them. Everybody leaned heavily on oral means for the intake of information. Publication of a poem meant its oral delivery by the author. Teachers gave out texts, commented on variants and discussed the figures of speech, wit and decorum of the author phrase by phrase. This involved providing etymologies of the words, the history of their various meanings and their social backgrounds and implications. Each student, therefore, made his own grammar, his own dictionary, rhetoric and commonplace book. Such was the practice in classrooms even in Shakespeare's day, a century after the invention of printing.

But, so far as the classroom was concerned, printing was decisive. Uniform texts became available along with grammars and dictionaries, not only of Latin but of Greek, Hebrew, and the vernacular tongues. Print made not only many more past texts available, but also large quantities of chronicle and historical matter which the medieval classroom could not possibly have found time to copy or discuss. From the point of view of previous education, this made a shambles. The flow of information shifted from wit, memory, and oral dialectics to multilingual erudition. When the main channel of information became the printed page, the critical powers of the young couldn't be trained in the same way. Print isolated the reader. The student who had formerly recited the lecture in a group and had then joined another group to discuss and dispute the points of the lecture was now alone with a text. In the same way, print isolated cultures, each in its own vernacular frame, where before all learning was in a single tongue.

Yet 16th century prose still retained many of the rapidly shifting perspectives of multiple levels of tone and meaning characteristic of group speech. It took two centuries of print to create prose on the page which maintained the tone and perspective of a single speaker. The individual scholar, alone with his text, had to develop habits of self-reliance which we still associate with the virtues of book culture. More and more learning was left to the unassisted industry of the individual. People were consumed by an "immoderate hydroptic thirst for humane learning and languages," in Donne's phrase, which went along with the first discovery of the smooth speedways of the printed page. No more stuttering pilgrimages through the crabbed columns of manuscript abbreviations. But it was a long time before people got to be at home with print. And by that time the newspaper page layout had begun to disturb the precarious equilibrium of 18th century book culture. The format of the 19th century newspaper page was like a dozen book pages set on a single sheet. The telegraph made this format the instantaneous global cross-section of a single day. This was no longer the book. Nor could the book stand up to this new cultural form born out of technology. The book tried to swallow this rival: Joyce in *Ulysses,* Eliot in *The Waste Land*—non-narrative epics which incorporate the newspaper art form.

The newspaper was merely the first of a quick succession of new information channels which challenged the cultural balance. But only the artists of our time have met or understood this challenge. With the arrival of print, Erasmus and his humanist colleagues saw exactly what had to be done in the classroom—and did it at once. But with the arrival of the press, nothing was done to accommodate its new modes of perception to an obsolete curriculum.

Education must always concentrate its resources at the point of major information intake. But from what sources do growing minds nowadays acquire most factual data and how much critical awareness is conferred at these points? It's a commentary on our extreme cultural lag that when we think of criticism of information flow we still use only the concept of book culture, namely, how much trust can be reposed in the words of the message. Yet the bias of each medium of communication is far more distorting than the deliberate lie.

**BLESS** THE ARTIST'S
# VISION
**OF THE**
# PRESENT

visible to him
because of the
freedom from
the constant or
# STABILIZED
# ENVIRONMENT

**BLESS** THOMAS KUHN'S **STRUCTURE** OF **SCIENTIFIC REVOLUTIONS** for bridging art and science beyond the **HOPES OF C. P. SNOW**

The format and tone of some press styles may make the very concept of truth irrelevant. The most urgent and reliable facts presented in this way are a travesty of any reality. The technological format of the *New York Times* is far more significant than any single report it could ever print. Its well known motto, "All the news that's fit to print," could very well be the text for any comic show. Editorial policy is of minute effect compared to the art form of the page itself. Until we understand that the forms projected at us by our technology are greatly more informative than any verbal message they convey, we're going to go on being helpless illiterates in a world we made ourselves.

We could do for the classroom what Erasmus did for the classroom of his day. We could make it the matrix of a cultural flowering much greater than that of the Elizabethan Age. For we possess, and to some degree already experience, the facts of media cross-fertilization. Great eras of culture occur when a large area of oral experience is invaded by a visual medium, or vice versa. For the Elizabethans, the whole folk wisdom of oral culture, centuries of oral disputation, and a huge backlog of vocal music were cross-fertilized by the printed page. A rich auditory heritage was exposed via a visual medium.

Today we live in the world's greatest period of culture, for the oral heritages of all cultures are being poured through visual traditions to the enrichment of all.

Just as history begins with writing, so it ends with TV. Just as there was no history when there was no linear time sense, so there is post-history now when everything that ever was in the world becomes simultaneously present to our consciousness.

Printing increased the scope of historical awareness; telegraphy and TV completed the process by making the past twenty-four hours or the past twenty-four millennia equally present. Media themselves act directly toward shaping our most intimate self-consciousness.

Freud commented on the insults heaped on man since the Renaissance. He suggested that all the discoveries made by man in recent centuries have automatically, as it were, become techniques for debunking. He saw psychoanalysis as a total invasion of privacy and meeting resistance because of its deep wound to human pride. From one point of view, it's possible to look at psychoanalysis as merely a recent by-product in a long series of cultural revolutions. One equivalent of psychoanalysis might be X-ray photography. Psychology without walls, on one hand; biology without walls, on the other.

Patrick Geddes noted:
*"Our Western civilization is based on Greek civilization which was essentially composed of city states. The spread of Roman roads led to their conquest and exploited and exhausted all regions into the metropolitan maw. When the roads were broken down the regions and cities of the Middle Ages returned to a separate though interdependent way of life . . ."*

The Roman road which represented a great improvement in the means of communication knocked down the physical and cultural walls of ancient cities. But the road was made feasible by writing, papyrus and the wheel. Until written messages could easily and cheaply be committed to a light and transportable medium, the road appears not to have offered many attractions to the organizers of armies, states and empires. This is a theme explored by the late Harold Innis, the economic historian of the Fur Trade, the railway and the cod fisheries. When the explorations of Innis brought him to the subject of the pulp and paper industries, he found himself compelled to extend his researches to the trade routes of the mind and of public opinion. So that willy-nilly he became the pioneer of the social and political effects of the media of communication. His historical researches had assured him many times that there cannot be any technological or physical change in the means of intercommunication that is unaccompanied by spectacular social change. A new medium is like the trumpet at the battle of Jericho.

Even a casual look at the media changes of recent centuries bears Innis out. Printing the Bible in the 15th century meant religion without walls. But unexpectedly it raised the towering walls of vernacular nationalism and individualism, for print upset corporate and liturgical worship. Although printing was the first mass medium, technologically considered, it isolated the reader and the student as never before. It shifted the stress in education and in the classroom from oral to written and visual instruction. Moreover, while print was the enemy of architecture, painting and music as these arts had been cultivated previously, it made possible the spread of information at least. Colonial America could not import plastic culture from Europe but it could print books and news.

By the time of the power press in the early 19th century, the newspapers were rapidly changing the character of politics by creating public opinion. In a new country like America the new medium of the press created the first instance of a state founded on public opinion. English political forms, predating the press, still depend much less on public opinion, as do those of Canada.

The urgency of collecting and speeding news as accelerated by the power press, had, as is well known, a great effect on the development of roads and railways. But the advent of the telegraph seemed suddenly to reduce the globe to the proportions of a town. The telegraph is a device of instantaneity which knocks down all cultural walls. The telegraph produces that patchwork quilt of global cross-section which we take for granted now on every page of the newspaper. As much as the Roman road, the telegraph was a remover of walls. And the natural consequence was diplomacy without walls.

Perhaps the effect of the telegraph has been, like that of later media, to break down the division between our inner and outer worlds, so that the reader of the newspaper accepts the newspaper not so much as a highly artificial image *having some correspondence to reality* as he tends to accept it as reality itself. Perhaps the effect is for the media to substitute for reality just in the degree to which they become virtuoso of realistic detail.

The telegraph was not just an extension of print. It is not the mechanization of writing but the electrification of writing. The movie was the mechanization of photography as TV was the electrification of images. The movie is another means of rolling up the mat of the external world in order to reveal it inside movie walls as a night-dream of the day world. The movie is to the novel what the novel was to the newspaper. And just as news photography knocked down some of the vernacular walls which still foster the passions of nationalism, so the movie knocked down the walls of individualism created by print. It also attacked the walls partitioning our dream and waking lives, and altered our sense of time and history by making all times and places immediately *present*.

## The order in which these changes occurred chronologically is not entirely their technological order of development.

Technically, the telegraph was far in advance of the movie or writing with moving images. And the telephone is in advance of the phonograph technically because the phonograph is merely the mechanization of speech and sound whereas the telephone is the electrification of speech, as the telegraph was the electrification of writing. But with the telephone came speech without walls.

## About the same time there arrived the motor-car, the home without walls.

Meanwhile, the world of pictorial advertising was presenting the skin you love to touch or the boudoir without walls. Though to our present experience of super-real nylon-covered surfaces the era of the photographic skin seems quaintly dated. Visual glamour now renders love without skin and photographic reporting or violence crescendoes without bodies.

One classic principle can be
seen operating clearly in all
matters related to the
development of the media of
communication. Namely,
that while any given form is
latent or incomplete in its
expression, it manifests itself
under its opposite. With
radio and TV we come to a
striking illustration of this
principle. The electronic or
vacuum tube first manifested
its powers in the acoustic
sphere but did not achieve
full expression until TV.
Radio is to the ear what
television is to the eye: the
instantaneous record and
transmission of sight
and sound.

please the **marxists**

for their **DEVOTION** to the

# REVOLUTION

that took place in our

# SERVICE ENVIRONMENTS

over a century ago.

# bless the
# pueblo episode

## for compressing in

## mythic FORM

## the entire syndrome of

# ELECTRONIC
# MAN

## reconquered by the

# iLLiTErATE

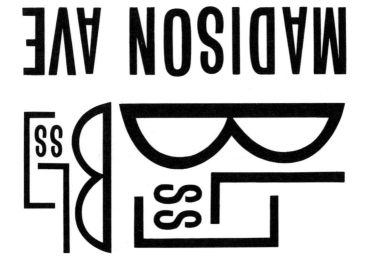

# MADISON AVE

FOR RESTORING THE

## magical art

OF THE

# CAVEMEN

TO

# SUBURBIA

Television, in sensorial terms, takes a large leap towards reassembling all the elements of interpersonal discourse which were split apart by writing and by all the intervening artificial media. For language itself is an acoustic medium which incorporates gesture and all the various combinations of sensuous experience, in a single medium of sound. Writing was probably the greatest cultural revolution known to us because it broke down the walls between sight and sound. Writing was a visualizing of the acoustic which split off or abstracted one aspect of speech, setting up a cultural disequilibrium of great violence. The dynamism of the Western world may well proceed from the dynamics of that disequilibrium. If so, our present stage of media development suggests the possibility of a new equilibrium. Our craving today for balance and an end of ever-accelerating change, may quite possibly point to the possibility thereof. But the obvious lesson of all this development for education seems to me both simple and startling. If our new media constitute so complete a range of expressiveness as both to enhance and almost to supplant speech itself, then we have moved into the period of post-literacy. If our present means of exploring and presenting the human past are such as to make simultaneously present all kinds of human pasts, then we have moved into the period of post-history. Not that we are to be deprived of books any more than of ancient manuscripts. But it is plain that our new culture is not going to lean very heavily on any one means of encoding experience or of representing reality. Already we are accustomed to a concert of the arts, of the sensuous channels and of the media. And in this respect we shall resemble pre-literate and pre-historic societies in the inclusiveness of our awareness.

That means also that we shall tend as they did towards homogeneity both of experience and organization. Perhaps, therefore, we have in our post-literacy come to the age of the classroom without walls.

It was very hard at first for the contemporaries of Erasmus to grasp that the printed book meant that the main channel of information and discipline was no longer the spoken word or the single language. Erasmus was the first to act on the awareness that part of the new revolution would be felt in the classroom. He put the old oral scholasticism into his *Adagia* and *Similia*. The same situation confronts us. We are already experiencing the discomfort and challenge of classrooms without walls, just as the modern painter has to modify his techniques in accordance with art reproduction and museums without walls. We can decide either to move into the new wall-less classroom in order to act upon our total environment, or to look on it as the last dike holding back the media flood. Let us consider that the flow of information into the student mind (and our own as well) which was once oral, and then printed, could easily be controlled in the classroom. Today only a tiny trickle of the information flow into the student mind can be accounted for in the classroom. For every fact or attitude which the teacher can initiate or direct, the visual and auditory environment provides many thousands of facts and experiences.

## FACED WITH INFORMATION OVERLOAD, WE HAVE NO ALTERNATIVE BUT PATTERN-RECOGNITION.

In a word, the cultural content approach is futile, even granting that it is preferable. To try to defend our civilization against itself by trying either to warn or to encourage the young about the surrounding chaos and vulgarity would be like the Eskimo trying to defend his culture against ours by taking a vow of silence. Our own history and our own methodology stand ready at hand to advise us in the present very dramatic climax. We must maximize rather than minimize the various features of our new media. It's easy now to see that they are not mere vehicles for already achieved experience and insight. We have moved far beyond mechanization. Let us not lose ourselves by supposing that we have merely to contend with new forms of mechanization. Radio and TV aren't new ways of handling manuscript and book culture. The motor-car wasn't a substitute for the horse. It did what the horse could never do. Radio and TV aren't audio-visual aids to enhance or to popularize previous forms of experience. They are new languages. We must first master and then teach these new languages in all their minute particularity and riches. In so doing we have available on an unprecedented scale the resources of comparison and contrast. We can compare the same play or novel or poem or news story as it's changed artistically in passing into the movie form, the stage, the radio and TV. We can note the precise qualities of each medium as we would compare the various degrees of effectiveness of a thought in Greek or French or English. This is what the young are doing sloppily and helplessly outside the classroom every day. This holds their attention automatically as the classroom does not.

In the electronic age as the media begin to dwarf nature, nature imitates art more and more. Oscar Wilde records his amazement at finding London drawing-rooms over flowing with long-necked, pale, auburn-haired women where, before the paintings of Rossetti and Burne-Jones, such women had never been seen. Today that is normal. Every movie and every issue of Vogue breezily sets out to revamp not only our clothes but our physiology. Such is the amount of power available today that the boundaries between art and nature have disappeared. Art has substituted for nature, and various new political regimes naturally tend to act on these assumptions. We have as little doubt about our ability to control global climate as the climate of opinion.

In such an age, with such resources, the walls of the classroom disappear if only because everybody outside the classroom is consciously engaged in national and international educational campaigns. Education today is totalitarian because there is no corner of the globe or of inner experience which we are not eager to subject to scrutiny and processing. So that if the educator old-style feels that he lives in an ungrateful world, he can also consider that never before was education so much a part of commerce and politics. Perhaps it is not that the educator has been shouldered aside by men of action so much as he has been swamped by high-powered imitators. If education has now become the basic investment and activity of the electronic age, then the classroom educator can recover his role only by enlarging it beyond anything it ever was in any previous culture. We cannot hope simply to retain our old prerogatives. Our bridges are gone and the Rubicon is yet to cross! We have either to assume a large new role or to abdicate entirely. It is the age of paratroopers.

Yes, we must substitute an interest in the media for the previous interest in subjects. This is the logical answer to the fact that the media have substituted themselves for the older world. Even if we should wish to recover that older world we can do it only by an intensive study of the ways in which the media have swallowed it. And no matter how many walls have fallen, the citadel of individual consciousness has not fallen nor is it likely to fall. For it is not accessible to the mass media.

# BLESS L.B.J.

FOR HIS
## STERN
STANCE
ON THE
# SHIP OF STATE
obsessed by the
# TURBULENCE
of
# PAST EVENTS

There is an Oxford college that memorialized the life-long devotion of one of its servants by the inscription:

HE KNEW HIS PLACE

In the semi-feudal world of Oxford that remark has none of the sinister or sneering quality that it naturally evokes in democratic ears. England is still a land in which the highest gentry and the lowly Cockney share a set of tribal loyalties that exclude the possibility of personal ambition or private goals. At both of these social extremes there is an assumption of total involvement in role that renders the striving for social or commercial success quite meaningless.

The self-effacement of the artist as catalyst, a surrender to process and ritual that is necessary to the role of actor or scientist or sleuth, creates in turn in the audience a feeling of immediate association with corporate power.

The involvement in role creates the image that is collective process.

Beaudelaire's *Hypocrite lecteur, mon semblable, mon frère* is itself an image that compresses the entire process in question. It is the recognition that there is no more division between the poet and his audience, between producer and consumer. The reader puts on the audience as his corporate or tribal mask. The audience creates the author as the author shapes the awareness of the audience.

As Stephen phrases it at the end of his
*Portrait of the Artist as a Young Man:*

> Welcome, O Life! I go to
> encounter for the millionth
> time the reality of experience
> and to forge in the smithy
> of my soul the uncreated
> conscience of my race.

This passage is the correlative or *ricorso* of
the first page that traverses the sensory
labyrinth of cognition. For it is by retracking
the process of cognition that our century
has recovered the power to suspend
judgement and to achieve an inclusive
consciousness. To transform ourselves
into probes and to abandon the traditional
visual obsession with fixed point of view
are the necessary prelude to extending not
just our nerves but the symmetrical ratios
of consciousness into the environment.

It was the absence of the power to probe
or to observe the environment of his time
that misled Marx in his *Communist
Manifesto* (1848). What became the
nightmare of the Communist threat from
then till now was a misunderstanding of
events that had already occurred.

Marx was as much the victim of the rear-view mirror as his opponents. Both were blinded to the new environments of corporate services by the assumptions of centuries of printed laws and institutes. In 1848 *The Communist Manifesto* began with the statement:

## "A Spectre is Haunting Europe —the Spectre of Communism."

Naturally, when the working man could command the services of a world postal system, fast transport, and mass-produced books and newspapers, he had access in effect to multi-billion dollar services that no private wealth could command for itself. The Marxists spent their lives trying to promote a theory after the reality had been achieved. What they called the class struggle was a spectre of the old feudalism in their rear-view mirror. But it served to distort the role of the new middle classes.

From 1850 to 1900 the clash of images in the Western mind was inspired by the industrial take-over of power from the gentry. Today the electric technology that retribalizes Western man takes over power from the world of mechanical industry and middle-class literacy. The mind of Karl Marx, completely conditioned by the eighteenth-century *literati* and the nineteenth-century applications of Gutenberg technology to mass-production, would have revolted from our global upsurge of tribal man.

Today all non-literate and semi-literate cultures, in the East and in the West, are "turned on" by the new electric environment. The literate cultures of the metropolitan middle class are "turned off" by the same means. Black Power is turned on; White Power is turned off. But the Negroes are as confused as the Japanese. Should they acquire Western literate and civilized techniques just when the West is going tribal-oriented, inward and non-literate? Black Power like Oriental Power is confronted with a total conflict of "goals" and images.

When images or identity, private or corporate, are confused, the natural response is blind violence. Such violence is never a quest for a goal but for an image.

# This was the HORROR of Hitler

Turned on tribally by radio, the Germans violently sought a new identity to match their new psychic dimension. They dissipated this new resource in a war retrospective in its goals. They used the mechanical technology of the nine-teenth century in the delusion of meeting a twentieth-century destiny.

Their confusion of images and goals is matched in every other sphere of the recent past and present. Radio turned on the American Negro in the 1920's, creating a totally new tribal culture for the only country in the world that was based on and formed by literate technology. American politics, education and business are the greatest monument to the civilizing and specializing power of the printed word. That is why the image of American identity resulting from this involvement in visual and literate culture is naturally hardest hit by the current electric technology. For instant electronic structures, both in themselves and in their extended psychic and social effects, are antithetic to visual and literate culture. When information is simultaneous from all directions at once, the culture is auditory and tribal, regardless of its past or its concepts. Hence the panic confusion in American education, business and politics alike.

All our teen-agers are now tribal. That is, they recognize their total involvement in the human family regardless of their personal goals or backgrounds. Their recognition of the uniform sphere of the electronic information environment renders obvious the *squareness* of all previous arrangements. But even American businesses are split in the same way about whether to pursue visual goals or to create environmental images. This is the crisis of American politics. Candidates are now aware that all policies and objectives are obsolete. Perhaps there is some comfort to be derived from the fact that NASA scientists are in the same dilemma. While pursuing the Newtonian goals of outer space, they are quite aware that the inner dimensions of the atom are very much greater and more relevant to our century.

The Catholic church is in the same dilemma. Prepared to de-Romanize or to decentralize its bureaucracy under electronic pressure, eager to revise its liturgy for greater participation, it is now caught in a doctrinal conflict with the dynamics of a great tradition of literacy that it has always accepted without understanding.

When we put satellites around the planet, Darwinian Nature ended. The earth became an art form subject to the same programing as media networks and their environments. The entire evolutionary process shifted, at the moment of Sputnik, from biology to technology. Evolution became not an involuntary response of organisms to new conditions but a part of the consensus of human consciousness. Such a revolution is enormously greater and more confusing to past attitudes than anything that can confront a mere culture or civilization.

# THE
# IVORY TOWER
## BECOMES
# THE CONTROL TOWER
## OF
# HUMAN NAVIGATION